THE BUSINESS OF LIFE

THE BUSINESS OF LIFE

101 ANSWERS TO TOUGH QUESTIONS

VAIBHAV MALOO

PAN

First published 2023 by Pan
an imprint of Pan Macmillan Publishing India Private Limited
707 Kailash Building
26 K. G. Marg, New Delhi 110001
www.panmacmillan.co.in

Pan Macmillan, The Smithson, 6 Briset Street, Farringdon, London EC1M 5NR
Associated companies throughout the world
www.panmacmillan.com

ISBN 978-81-19300-08-2

The views expressed in this book are the author's own and the facts reported by him have been verified by the publisher to the extent possible. The publisher hereby disclaims any liability to any party for loss, damages or disruptions caused by the same.

1 3 5 7 9 8 6 4 2

Typeset in Electra LT Std by R. Ajith Kumar, New Delhi
Printed and bound in India by Replika Press Pvt. Ltd.

This book is dedicated to all who want to succeed in life; it is written in an effort to help my readers get past the chaos of life.

CONTENTS

Our World 49

Society, Culture and Religion 105

PREFACE

When one has free time, one has a chance to ponder and deliberate. However, with technological advances and our growing addiction to our phones, while food for thought has increased manifold, free time has terribly reduced. When I was growing up, things were less digital and slower, but for the subsequent generations, things have drastically changed. They have to constantly advance and be at the top of their game. Children today also need to be taught differently, involving the frequent help of technology.

I am a thinker and am often found reading and writing on flights and in coffee shops. You can find me driving around in Mumbai, gathering my thoughts. I got the idea of writing this book on one such long drive. This book has given me the opportunity to put my views across to you, the reader, in the hope that you might something useful within its pages.

The book comprises essays on various topics that are of interest to ordinary people like me, who are either confused about what they should believe in or how they should think structurally about their beliefs. The human mind tends to wander and ponder, and I have penned my thoughts in the hope of finding and sharing the answers to a range of questions.

My views may differ from the readers' on various subjects, and that variety is the beauty of life. It signifies the richness of everyone's experiences. While I have tried to be as blunt as possible in today's climate of strict checks on radicalism, and I think I am a political centrist, I hope my views don't offend anyone. Please bear in mind that the views expressed here are personal and in no way reflect the views of any entity affiliated with me.

Freedom of speech and expression is a fundamental right in India, and I believe it should be a basic human right everywhere. I think, authoritarianism is soon coming to an end globally, and people's voices are finally being heard, enabling them to grow and prosper without fear, to rise above the mundane and hope for a free future for their children and grandchildren. I'm simply a small part of this global crowd.

I hope this book finds you in good stead, and you enjoy reading it.

BUSINESS

001 | Why do governments facilitate business growth?

As someone from a business family, I was taught the ropes of the trade by my family from an early age. During my formative years, dinner table discussions came with opportunities to learn the basics. An avid reader and observer, I believe that there is nothing like practical knowledge. Not even B-schools and degree courses can teach one the basics of business. It boils down to common sense and application.

Every large business, when broken down, is the same. Take the computer hardware business for example. It requires procuring microchips, durable plastic, insulated wires, plugs, mobile applications, software licences and so many other things. Can you imagine the boost Apple Inc must have given to businesses manufacturing these parts across the world? Then imagine the accessories that each Apple computer comes with – covers, chargers, power packs, add-ons – the list is long. A trillion-dollar market capitalization creates many a billion.

A trillion dollars doesn't seem like an impossibly high figure anymore. Global oil companies, mining giants and Big Tech, including Microsoft, Facebook, Google and Berkshire Hathaway, have all upped their game in a bid to reach the new milestone – the trillion-dollar mark. No matter what the leadership says, I can assure you most of them do care about their company's stock prices. The stock exchanges have given a new impetus to many companies. Keeping in mind the fact that every company has an ecosystem of multiple stakeholders: suppliers, customers, employees and more, the revised targets have led to an overall improvement in various matrices across the board. Employment goes up and with it the standards of products and services.

Some diversified conglomerates – flourishing and profit-making groups of companies – that are in the limelight in India are the age-old Tata, Essar, Mahindra, Reliance, RPG and Aditya Birla. As for the West, we have General Electric, Virgin, Trump, etc. So specialized or diversified, corporations and/or family-owned businesses, at their core they are all just that – businesses.

Business growth and development are pivotal for any economy, and cross-border co-dependence is unavoidable in the age of globalization. It is evident that when a recession hits, everyone gets affected. However, all targets can be achieved if we create a solid framework and an environment conducive for businesses to operate and grow in, be it higher tax collections, more employment or better products and services.

The far-right or proponents of extreme political ideologies, I feel, often slow down business development and, in turn, growth and prosperity. It is important to understand their sentiments, but nothing is more important than health, wellbeing, economic prosperity and happiness which can only be brought along by a people's and society's progress. Too much pride and entanglement with local issues often get in the way of progressive policies and deter industrial growth. In the past, this has been the reason for slow progress in many economies. The Chinese government adopted a leftist approach, and look at how fast their economy has grown. Look at the progress of USA, Japan and the European nations as well that have facilitated the growth of businesses. Though not as extremist as China, their economies have grown rapidly as well. India is also following suit. In fact, the country is already showing signs of prosperity, and I laud Prime Minister Narendra Modi and his leadership for this.

The last two prime ministers of India – Dr Manmohan Singh and Atal Bihari Vajpayee – deserve a fair share of the credit. They were reformists and took courageous steps, with maturity and astuteness, towards the economic growth of the country. Today, our country is growing at one of the fastest rates compared to any major economy in the world.

Businesses generate employment and thus bring in an abundance of resources. Although there is a strong dependence on agriculture, and this is true for most nations, trade forms the backbone of the gross domestic product (GDP). The more the spending capacity of a nation, the better the focus on health services, education and research. Propelling industrial growth is also the best way forward to solving problems related to poverty and increasing income gaps. This is applicable to all economies, regardless of their size.

The challenges that face business growth, however, are greater in places that have less skilled labour. Education must be brought to every doorstep of in the world to make up for this lack. Technology adoption has become a key parameter in determining efficiency in an increasingly automated world and thus must be promoted. Behind each giant spring up many more, and behind them, some more.

I just want to add here that the bias against family-run businesses must end. Sometimes high stakeholder interest in a well-established business can lead to superior performance, and a well-instilled corporate governance mechanism is a major prerequisite. Europe is full of family-owned brands that have been running successfully for centuries. My own businesses are both family-owned and diversified and, unfortunately, I can't recall many success stories of companies otherwise – that's the harsh reality. There is a shared pool of resources, a capitalistic approach to life, discreet knowledge and other factors that also come into play within this setup. Of course, on the flip side there is crony capitalism and nepotism too, which exist in imperfect economies. But the world isn't a utopia yet.

002 | Should we remove hierarchy with a hands-on approach in business?

Most organizations are hierarchical. There is a top-down chain of command, and people work within the ambit of their designated titles and positions. I think that's a pragmatic way of organizing a company with a large number of employees, when they are required to execute things in a specific manner. However, there are ways in which the inner circle of chief strategists and CXOs can function better. The top leadership shouldn't forget that each employee has infinite potential and that harnessing it could be a source of organizational growth.

In the case of Enso, which is a mid-sized organization in terms of employees, employees often skip the chain of command to offer valuable advice. As a result, I find that the corporate office in many ways is a think tank, replete with creativity and big ideas, even outside the cabins of the big bosses. The secret behind this is that we, as the promoters, give our employees the respect and freedom to be honest and express views openly, irrespective of hierarchy. This approach has taught me something very meaningful. Every individual's power of mind is infinite, and if you can harvest that, your company will grow from strength to strength. And while every field is different, drawing out the full potential of every member of an organization is better than having them do the bare minimum. That's a great underutilization of human potential and can be demotivating for collective performance in the longer run. At Enco, we often hand out bonuses and employee achievement awards to incentivize performance. Being heard is a sure-shot way of adding to the motivation level of employees.

I don't think the chain of command needs to be enforced everywhere. This comes with a disclaimer that nobody should misuse their access across the board, of course, and that's why enterprises must hire only quality individuals with merit. Positions that come with job descriptions give way to structure and enable the allocation of responsibility feasibly. But each of these positions should come with a certain freedom for the hired persons to maximize their potential, not just perform their obligatory duties.

There should be a palpable team spirit channelled towards a common purpose. Even if that purpose is something as simple as increasing sales, for example, the right strategy, as well as the bigger picture, should be made clear to all concerned. That will enable decision-making and align everyone with the leadership's vision. This is vital. Corporate strategy is very important, and the game of management must be played nicely by senior leaders.

003| How can you build your brand's ethos?

To me, marketing is all about obsessively and compulsively thinking about the most effective ways of communicating the brand's ethos and transforming lives. You have to keep pushing out the message until it really feels like you are known and have recall value among your target population, whether local, regional, national or global.

Create the best product, do your best and don't rest till you are known to be the best. A good logo is a must. It should be one that attracts attention. A solid brand should be able to speak for itself in such a way that a representative does not have to spend time explaining to people what they do; people familiar with the brand will know it. Its image should be global, green and transparent. Investing in a brand's ethos is an investment in the future of the company and is to be guarded like a priceless asset.

When I think of a solid brand, I think of Tata, Rolls-Royce, Bentley, McKinsey, Hermes, Rolex, Microsoft, Apple and Google. All of them have stood the test of time, in terms of product quality, service and management. Bear in mind that the journey of building a strong brand begins from building a strong product; that the latter will decide the strength of your finances.

The many stakeholders of your product or company are part of the value creation circle, and they should all be proud to wear the badge of your brand image alongside theirs. A possible investor, to be specific, also buys into your brand, and I don't mean just the intellectual property rights (IPR) of the logo, but the company's ethos and its past hard work, which are a part of the brand legacy.

While attending Carnegie Mellon University's Tepper School of Business for my undergraduate degree in business administration, marketing was my favourite subject. I got a solid 'A', along with what might have been a good recommendation from my professor, who told me that I was in the best place for studying business. I quietly agreed. I remember working on the marketing plan for the Segway, which was a new product released at the advent of the millennium. Since then, I have loved marketing.

It is an abstract art. It may seem like a science because of the number of frameworks and structures involved, as well as the many theories, but a mix of a lot of things in random proportion is again an art.

One recalls certain names because they are easy to remember, and that should also be your marketing mantra. The ethos of your brand should be simple. It should be communicated through branding exercises that convey loyalty and care to consumers.

Just as a business requires common sense more than structured frameworks, marketing also requires ground-level thinking and, often, just like business, this art also requires some testing of the market. You can start with social media, which offers entirely free platforms to test and showcase your marketing skills.

Today, people think of themselves as brands when often they are the product themselves. If you want to become a brand, your skill set in your chosen field as well as being noncontroversial is key. You must invest in yourself. Personal and professional sacrifices are sometimes directly linked to your success and that of your brand(s). With time and experience, one might get into multiple industries and manage several brands. Thought leadership, in addition, creates another brand, which is you yourself. That leaves a narrow window to err because you are in the spotlight 24x7. These are hard choices that you have to make as a leader. But one point must always be clear – you must do what you love, as you are at some level going to be a product of your career and choices.

A brand's ethos can be built on pillars of a strong past and present and the promise of a bright future. Keep it plain and simple. I have always opted for green brand associations, be it with sporting events, celebrities or even influencers. A lot of hustling can take you far. Keep at it and watch your pockets – don't overspend. There are creative ways to do things at a lower cost. Let the brand ethos get built gradually while sticking to a path of endless service through your offerings.

004 | How easy is it to go global?

'Act local, think global', a slogan that was once used by marketing experts the world over, applies most to running global businesses. In India, where I live, many foreign brands have entered the scenes. If these brands thought that they could sweep in with their global identity and do well here, or any market for that matter, they would have been right until a few years ago. Today's consumer, however, is conscious, smart and has no dearth of choices. Thus, for deeper market penetration and increased market share, businesses are required to adapt – their products and services and their communication to the customers – as per local needs in order to strike a chord.

The challenge for companies entering new markets is not to win over global citizens, people who have widely travelled and are early movers in the adoption cycles, but to win over the locals, who aren't that exposed to the outside world. All big enterprises, right from Google to Amazon to Facebook, have had to launch local advertising campaigns in India to win over the majority of people living in small towns and cities, who hadn't adopted their platforms yet. The middle-class consumer today is very smart and looks for value for money spent, while those with a higher disposable income look for superior quality. In the latter case, there is a niche created, and that is a higher segment market.

Let's take the example of Unilever. The global company has an Indian arm called Hindustan Unilever. It offers various FMCG products, the names of which are different from those that are sold in, say, a country like Thailand. These names are designed to target people in a similar income stratum across geographies. The company realizes that all these people need to be won over for the brand to take on a leading market position. The pricing strategy has to be in accordance with consumer income and sometimes, the products need to be altered to suit market needs.

Often, we think of going global as a huge leap, but in some cases, it could be cheaper to operate from certain other countries than your home country. It's all about your understanding of global business and the efficacy of your communication skills. You must be able to sell your offerings to foreign consumers. By going global, you may sometimes gain from the price differential in the monetary value of goods and services in that country. The cost of setting up an office, hiring staff and local administration has to be sustainable in the beginning, but if your plan fails and your business is unable to attract people, you may have to shut shop and write off the investment. One must also factor in and plan for the worst-case scenario at every step.

There could be many barriers to running a business arm in a foreign country, one of the biggest being government regulations. Another challenge is corruption. Walmart backed out of India when there were reports of widespread corruption. It did not want to risk being held accountable in their home country, as their global business and reputation would suffer. The Indian government did not allow sole entry into India for retail, and hence, Walmart is not in India.

We see, therefore, that there are multiple hurdles to

entry into foreign markets, and one has to be astute while undertaking international expansion. Often, entering new markets requires deep pockets and a time commitment. Customization shows that you care, so add that to the list too.

The ultimate secret of marketing, however, – something that no one can rig – is word of mouth. Even though packaging and branding are important, nothing is more crucial than a product's quality and customers' heartfelt testimonials.

005| Who is a visionary?

There is a difference between the ordinary and the great. Sheikh Mohammed raised Dubai; Bill Gates, a young prodigy, never looked back after the launch of his disruptive Windows; Apple Inc. under Steve Jobs transformed the world of electronics and continues to do so; Ratan Tata redefined management; Jack Welch made General Electric what it is today. These are just some of the great leaders who got where they did only by undertaking some amount of risk. We must bear in mind that while being risk-averse is important, we should not be afraid to take calculated risks if time and money permit.

To make it to extraordinary heights, one has to embrace risks. Education often teaches you structured ways of thinking, but that definitely doesn't seem to be enough to be successful in business and life. Mark Zuckerberg, who founded Facebook, left Harvard prematurely and yet made it to the Forbes' list of billionaires at an age when most people are still learning. One has to dream big and scale heights, even in the face of criticism and roadblocks.

This clearly shows that having the vision to scale globally, thinking out of the box and creating something, as well as having the conviction and grit to deliver, is not everyone's cup of tea. If you also have discipline in addition to it all, your vision is likely to translate into reality.

I firmly believe that education is very important – it's your insurance and could be an umbrella on a rainy day. It can also be a source of your pride, but the best people have won at life with simple common sense.

We have so many schools and college dropouts who have made it big – Dhirubhai Ambani, Gautam Adani, Steve Jobs, Bill Gates, Richard Branson, Mark Zuckerberg and so on. What they all have had in common is a powerful vision that resonated with their consumers' needs and the ability to translate that vision into excellent products by sheer focus and application for their offering into reality.

006 | What value do women add in a professional space?

I have realized that one can be innovative with organizational structuring to create a mix of management positions for ensuring an efficient organization. But there still seems to be glaring lack of women in these managerial positions in companies and establishments worldwide. Even if they aren't blatantly objectified and disrespected, women are not given their due. How and why is this still ongoing?

I think if a company or a group runs like a machine, the output can be great in terms of its financial figures, reputation and brand image. This depends on the management of the company, which differs from business to business.

However, management, historically speaking, has been patriarchal. For example, I often wonder why the designation 'chairwoman' isn't widely used like its male counterpart 'chairman'. In the rare occasion of a woman leading a board, the term used to denote her position is 'chairperson'. Similarly, instead of 'businesswoman' being used for a woman running a business, the neutral term used is 'businessperson'. This reflects that the attitude of society is far from matriarchal.

Women can be very valuable in running any institution or organization. To think about it logically, half of the world's population is female. In my opinion, there are certain physiological differences between men and women, but that is usually to do with endurance for physical labour. Other than that, women can have a great impact on the workforce and should be involved in the professional world with the same gusto as men. Differences between the symbolism around masculinity and femininity should be avoided, focusing instead on humanity, which is foremost.

According to me, men and women should receive equal pay for equal work.

Opportunities for women to contribute to the workforce must increase, and today, many people are vocalizing their support for it. We live in an age where, on one hand, the Taliban is actively denying women basic human rights and banning them from attending universities, while on the other we have women Nobel laureates and world leaders who are setting new benchmarks. There is no reason why the latter should not be the case everywhere. It's just a matter of time before the restraints put on women and girl children across the world are shattered.

Universal efforts are being made to educate children to secure hundred per cent literary rates across the world, regardless of gender. Girls should be educated and allowed to work, so they can become strong, independent women, who no longer need to fight for fundamental rights and an equal place in society.

007| How efficient are family businesses?

Family-owned businesses have been the norm for a long time. In fact, the earliest businesses in the world's history were entirely managed by families. Among the famous family-run businesses of today are Bombardier, Heineken, Walmart, Ford Motors, Glencore, Red Bull, Koch Industries, Comcast, Airtel, Tata Group, Mahindra Group, Wipro, Trump Organization and many more.

What I see as noteworthy is that interest in these businesses is still high, as the people behind the scenes are major shareholders. Thus, investors too are bullish about these businesses, sometimes even more than professionally run firms, as there is often higher accountability and stability to fall back on.

Stock markets look green if a company is doing well, is managed transparently and has above-board governance. This is often the case for family-run businesses. Succession planning usually comprises one or more family members, and they also take up key positions in management. Family-owned businesses form a crucial part of India's business culture, although a new wave of complete professionalizing has begun. Many are still averse to it, and instead maintain the status quo. Part of the reason is that most business owners want their children, who often hold fancy degrees from

B-schools, to succeed them and take the trade to newer zeniths.

I strongly feel that family businesses should be a topic covered in the B-school curriculum, as there are many vital case studies and much evidence in support of such ventures that is worth studying. The 'Ownership Project' at my alma mater Oxford University's Saïd Business School is an excellent example that allows studying the cause and effect of family-owned enterprises.

People heading large family businesses often amass large fortunes and create such a profile for themselves that gives them the opportunity to participate in key government and industrial advisory boards and committees, making a difference in society and their country. Of course, it goes without saying that citizens who excel in their chosen fields and who pay taxes on time also deserve to have a say in society.

There are always great philanthropists who turn to charity, and we are in the midst of a new wave of positive development in this direction. The Giving Pledge, founded by Bill Gates and Warren Buffet, is a charitable campaign for wealthy individuals who want to dedicate a majority of their fortune to philanthropic causes.

I strongly believe that serving society is the ultimate goal of doing business. Generating employment, paying taxes, supporting causes and delivering good tangible and intangible products and services help one be of use to society.

Ideas evolve across generations, and we all know of some centuries-old business houses that are still flourishing and reaching newer pinnacles, often following the wisdom of their forefathers. They say that money can corrupt, and if handed over to the next generation, it should be done with wise instructions and training so it's not lost. This is true, as wealth otherwise may be squandered away, as it was in the ancient Roman Empire.

I am not against luxury, for I believe that is one of the objectives of earning, but I do also believe in modest and respectable conduct and an impactful existence. Money can be a tool to improve lives, both yours and that of other human beings. Family businesses, too, hold great power to turn the tide and make a difference.

Conversely, sometimes a family holding majority shares of a company may refuse to issue fresh stocks. They do this to retain control, but it is often seen as a breach of interest of minority shareholders by the promoters and also stymies the growth of the organization. Hence the paradox in the case of listed companies – that they won't grow as the promoters won't allow themselves to be diluted – is a fallacy. It is imperative to do what's best for your trade, and that is what the board is there to ensure. However, with an ownership percentage of fifty-one and above, any board directive can be undone.

Business families spend years honing and grooming themselves to run their businesses, much like the princes and princesses of yesteryears who were groomed to take on kingdoms. They can be good at running the business if their interests are in the right place.

008 | Why should you try to be credible?

It is said that some things cannot be bought with money. Credibility, or the quality of being trustworthy, is one of them. We often see that people don't give enough importance to the quality of their product or service, which, in turn, reflects poorly on their entire company's credibility. You cannot cheat a customer, nor can you ever indulge in activities that might lead people to lose trust in you or your venture. People running a business must closely watch their dealings as well, as their conduct reflects on the entire company's credibility. Guidelines are often given out to other employees, advising them to maintain decorum even in their personal lives. But what some honchos forget is that their own misbehaviour outside work can sometimes come back to bite them at the workplace, so guard your personal behaviour and credibility.

If you promise something to your customers – say an offer, a product, a service or anything at all – you must aim to exceed their expectations. They say that your reputation precedes you. I've already stated that word of mouth is the strongest form of marketing. Some brands have been built as a result of years of hard work, and one small mistake can undo their entire reputation. Credible firms are very careful about who they deal with and what they do, and often forego opportunities that might put their credibility at risk. The pharmaceutical industry is therefore much dreaded, for a liability suit can ring the death knell for a company if found irresponsible. Investors are also wary of associating themselves with oil and gas projects to remain affiliated to green, sustainable businesses.

Companies that care about their image, and for which reputation is more sacred than spreadsheets inspire confidence and assurance among their customers towards their products and services. What can be trusted more easily is more likely to gain popularity.

A credible leader heading a firm does not backtrack from their words and instead goes out of their way to fulfil a commitment. The quality of staying true to your words is what ensures your personal credibility, and it goes a long way. Many successful businessmen are known to be greedy and often indulge in dealings where they may let down their business partners. Such people may make a quick buck, but they don't command the respect, name and prestige that their trustworthy counterparts enjoy. It is a bad trade-off. The road less travelled is bountiful, both in terms of the journey and the destination. Taking relationships seriously, both in business and personal life, is a good start for building a culture of honour among your comrades and kin. One must lead by example and inculcate an honourable outlook towards doing business and living among neighbours. Love thy neighbour, they say.

Corporate diplomacy is not very different from global diplomacy. You have to invest in the goodwill of your company and amass acceptability. Politeness is a necessary behaviour. Not passing negative remarks about the competition, sticking to the spirit of the company, and more importantly, knowing that others are out there to make money too are essential traits of a credible businessman. So don't aim to swallow or destroy the competition. Run the show with a touch of grace and complacency, making an effort to do push yourself up, rather than pulling others down.

So personal diplomacy and then corporate/global diplomacy, in that order, should be the mantra for a leader who can get work done, stand shoulder to shoulder with countrymen and contribute to healthy nation- and planet-building, no matter your place of birth or residence.

009 | What is the logic behind diversification in business and is it a good practice?

They say that business acumen runs deep in the societies where families have run businesses for centuries. India has no dearth of such real-life success stories. These must be studied before creating MBA courses around the world.

Being from a business family and watching my father conduct his business gave me the confidence to follow in his footsteps. It often seems easy, but there is a lot behind businessmen, and they are honed over generations. Being from a modest business family and having learnt the ins and outs by reading a lot of books, I love sharing my conclusion – that diversification of businesses is not just about crony capitalism in a corrupt world. Let's hope that new and upcoming diversified businesses last, and that they become a part of the canon of stories of old money or generational wealth. We must invest in future generations, so our wealth and progeny grow in strength.

In India, there are many diversified conglomerates, which are basically groups of companies that engage in various areas of specialization that are often unrelated. These groups are usually family-owned but are run by elected or hired professionals. Some of these are listed companies, and are run under the same umbrella, using the same brand name, like the many companies under the Adani Group. Contrary to this model, there are companies that specialize in one niche and grow organically in that area, such as General Motors or Google. But there is a lot of diversification within this one chosen industry segment that these organizations may undertake. In such cases, the degree of diversification is smaller compared to that of other global groups such as General Electric and Virgin, two classic time-tested examples. In India, there are plenty of thriving conglomerates, which showcase the advantages of well-focussed and managed diversification.

In today's world of complex investor demands, the various units of a diversified group must adhere to corporate governance and transparency. Otherwise, they will just end up gaining a bad name and be known as being 'investor unfriendly'.

In the case of diversified groups, the group leaders also take up the leadership of the boards of their companies. This in turn acts as an impetus to grow promoter interest in their companies, as they are direct stakeholders.

This structure is supported by a management headquarters that manages all the companies under the umbrella using the same brand name. A small management fee may be charged to take care of the central cell expenses. Any branding applied to one company of the group automatically rubs off on the others, so the success of of all companies is tied together. Centralized control is important for managing performance, making key decisions and looking out for risks and threats. Each company in a group must also have its own independent management, comprising of field specialists. It is important to give them a free hand despite being under the ambit of the headquarters.

In the case of a common promoter, their equity in sub-companies or group companies must be held in a holding company or a trust for legal protection, and to ensure longevity. The beneficiary, in the case of a trust, could be a member of their family, a charitable cause or both. In the case of the former, one must be prudent about the selection of the jurisdiction, as it should be a strong one.

Interaction between management officials of individual companies within the group should be encouraged, and off-site visits and conferences should be organized from time to time by the group leaders at the headquarters. This helps keep up the spirit of everyone involved in the success story of the group and builds team spirit.

The code of conduct, as much as possible, should be the same across the group, as these values, which should be carefully thought through before penning down, can serve as the guiding principles for the entire workforce of the group. They should be universal and follow global standards. The local laws of operational regions may need to be reviewed before deciding on the work culture of offices on foreign shores.

Each company leader must be appraised periodically and apprised of the need to adhere to salient features of the company code of conduct. They are the ambassadors of your brand and must be heard as well. Insights from business professionals can be interesting, and there should always be room for refining your own thoughts and bouncing ideas, back and forth, that stem from individual experience and learning.

The advantage of not putting all your eggs in one basket by having a diversified group is that when required, the promoter headquarters can rescue a company at the end of a bad year.

Overall, I feel, diversified groups are an effective structure and exist for many advantageous reasons, including pre-existing surplus funds. If handled and managed well, they could create immense value for all stakeholders. The common cash pool is the secret, and the support of each company's resources can help the entire group or conglomerate at large. It takes a lot to succeed in one business, so the difficulty increases manifold when there are multiple businesses. However, diversified ventures are structure-friendly and easier to manage in the case of large families where more hands are involved in the business.

010 | Should businesses bother with tax avoidance and offshore structuring?

We often hear of businessmen wanting to evade taxes. To do this, they often consult tax specialists and come up with offshore structuring schemes based in countries that allow zero taxation. A few examples are the British Virgin Islands (BVI), Cyprus, Cayman Islands, Mauritius, Hong Kong, Panama, sub-jurisdictions of Dubai and Seychelles, among others. However, a person trying to avoid taxes cannot run their business smoothly and is often on the run, as there are very few tax-free jurisdictions where they can reside. Therefore, it's never a good idea to try to evade taxes.

A non-resident Indian or NRI doesn't necessarily have to pay taxes in India, but this is limited to personal taxation. There are detailed cases where this exemption applies, like spending a minimum number of days outside the country and overseas employment.

A special purpose vehicle (SPV) is a subsidiary company created for a specific purpose. In the case of SPV structuring, offshore companies being managed by offices in any taxable country need to pay taxes in that country, and in case the country doesn't levy taxes, then the business can essentially run tax-free. In Asia, Dubai is the best-known option for people who are seeking asylum from taxation.

However, if a person or a group of people running a

business reside in India, the US, the UK, Singapore or any other jurisdiction that levies taxes, then the company pays taxes in that country. It doesn't matter where the directors are from or where the shareholders are from – it's the management of the company, the SPV, that counts.

There are usually double taxation avoidance treaties in place between countries, and if key people running the show of a company have conflicting residencies, then they get tax credits worth the difference between the tax rates of the two territories. If they have paid in the country with higher taxation, then they have complied. If the company pays taxes nowhere and is being managed from a taxed location, then it is required to pay the entire taxation of that jurisdiction, and there is no escape.

I believe paying taxes is the responsible thing to do. A person is indeed as close to themselves as they are to their culture, as hypothesized by John Hooker, a Carnegie Mellon professor of international management. Thus, they would not want to live overseas to save tax. For me, paying taxes and living peacefully is the way to go. Bear in mind that there really isn't any route to bring tax-saved money in your offshore account back to the home country without paying taxes. The conclusion is that there is no escape from taxes other than a permanent domicile abroad.

011| Why should one pay taxes?

Paying taxes is the single biggest connection between a country and its people. Taxes are usually levied in exchange for governance, civic amenities, infrastructure, law enforcement, protection, legal cover and to provide all kinds of security and facilities to taxpayers. The biggest utility people and businesses have for a nation are the taxes paid by them, as the money is used to help nation-building. Tax paid by individuals is called income tax, while that paid by companies is called corporate tax. In addition to these two, other taxes can be levied by the country. In India, we have goods and services tax (GST), minimum alternative tax (MAT), customs duty, property tax, gift tax and so on.

In some countries, tax rates are very high. Businesses tend to view that as a deterrent and, as a result, tend to choose international structuring options. Keeping tax percentages low and reasonable is the surest way to get everyone to pay them. People, irrespective of where they hail from, have a habit of complaining about taxation and how the government doesn't do enough with the tax money. My personal view is that all changes may not be visible and that the government and may want to take care of a range of inconspicuous issues facing the country. Citizens should do their duty and pay taxes on time.

Evading taxes can have multiple implications, from

prosecution to compounded penalties, and one must be aware of the law of the land to make the right choices. For the longest time, I did not have clarity about taxation and the laws regarding them, but I consulted lawyers once we faced some income tax hurdles and now have a better idea. There is enough material available online about tax rules of various jurisdictions, but instead of blindly relying on that, always go by expert advice.

I strongly believe that the growth of small and medium enterprises (SMEs) should be encouraged by slashing their tax rates, as should be done for enterprises working on the production of renewable energy. Charitable trusts should be given complete relaxation. Globally, tax rates are revised every year as part of the annual budget, and people keep a close watch on them.

A country being rich or poor is not just a factor of its GDP or gross national product, but also depends on tax collections, as the money then is deployed to improve facilities. If you remove the smoke screen, you will see that countries function like companies being run to make profits.

For India, that has ongoing friction with its neighbours, Pakistan and China, the expenditure on defence runs into billions of dollars, which, I feel, can be avoided through meaningful diplomatic dialogue. It will also help restore healthy ties with our neighbours. That is in the interest of all economies. During his presidency, Donald Trump stated that the American defence budget was soaring, and yet he wanted to sit down with the leaders of Russia and China to end the arms race. My eyes lit up at that news, and I realized how a creative solution could solve all global issues. The hard-earned money of American taxpayers could be used to improve so many lives.

When people get back services and benefits from the government in return for taxes, they complain less. That is why we must vote, and vote wisely – a power given to the citizens of all democratic countries – and have governments live up to their end of the deal by making visible changes and earning those votes again.

012 | What really is the essence of a stock exchange?

An exchange is a platform through which people support businesses financially and make a fair share of capital gains in the process. Some of the earliest stock exchanges were the Amsterdam Stock Exchange and Frankfurt Stock Exchange, which began in the sixteenth century. While earlier an exchange was run manually, using handwritten notes and commitments, today's stock exchanges have become high-tech, with trading happening in split seconds. Among many things, the stock market was Europe's gift to commerce.

Modern-day billionaires are ranked as per their net worth, mostly based on the cumulative sum of the stock they own. While that is a good indicator as it is liquid and a fair value, I am a big fan of Warren Buffet's business model. Under his model, 'investment management', the net value of stock holding is also determined by means of underlying stocks, and money is also liquid in this way. However, this model is not easy to maintain and is prone to risks. Buffet has mastered the art of beating the markets, but not everybody can do that.

These days, companies list on one or more stock exchanges that trade actively, and their performance is determined by their profitability and dividend payouts as well as their future promise. There are thriving professions and businesses around the stock market: websites like

Bloomberg and Yahoo Finance, news channels like CNBC, financial dailies and other media that keep you abreast with the latest in the markets.

Investing in the stock markets is sometimes considered to be calculated gambling. The trick is to study the financial statements of companies, understand their corporate governance, combine that analysis with the daily intake of news and trends and then make investment decisions. Wise people don't trade daily but take long-term calls and then put capital into a company.

Stocks are liquid assets and can be monetized anytime, so if your choice of stocks is good, you can essentially sleep peacefully knowing that, even in case of a crisis, it will recover, and you can sell easily by putting a downside trigger price, saving yourself the grief of waiting for too long for it to recover, lest it fall below a threshold. Remember, in the long run, stock markets always go up in terms of indices graphs. Rarely do they dip in the long run.

Usually, companies that have stood the test of time are good investments. Companies with a reputation of long-term profitability are given the tag of blue-chip companies. The various indices belonging to stock markets are usually an average of the best stocks of that country, often derived from a formula.

I would say that the New York Stock Exchange (NYSE), nicknamed the Big Board, is the best and the largest exchange in the world in terms of market capitalization and trading infrastructure. It's where everyone wants to be.

Among the top exchanges by market capitalization and quality are NASDAQ, Japan Exchange Group, the Shanghai Stock Exchange and the Hong Kong Stock Exchange. The next five are the Euronext of the EU, which is based in

Amsterdam, the Shenzhen Stock Exchange, the London Stock Exchange (LSE), the Toronto Stock Exchange (TMX) and the Bombay Stock Exchange (BSE). Some exchanges, such as the NYSE, allow global listings, while some have reservations about them. These days, online trading is allowed for most exchanges, and all you need to trade is an account that is opened after some KYC (Know Your Client) details are provided and can be set up in a day. It's very easy to create a global portfolio in today's climate.

There are ancillary exchanges for new ventures, and these exchanges account for smaller companies, such as the Alternative Investment Market (AIM) in London. The Toronto Stock Exchange is a hub for mining and energy companies.

India has six active major exchanges:

1. The Bombay Stock Exchange (BSE)
2. The National Stock Exchange (NSE)
3. The Calcutta Stock Exchange (CSE)
4. The Metropolitan Stock Exchange (MSE)
5. The India International Exchange (India, INX)
6. NSE IFSC Limited (NSE International Exchange).

Stock markets, or financial markets, are amazing institutions, providing support and livelihood to brokers, firms, traders and many others, but one mustn't put all their eggs in one basket. By this I mean that people should maintain diversified portfolios in well-reputed, profitable firms with a good business model and take a long-term view of investing. They should analyse their investments after considering global trends and understand the parameters influencing the market, both external and internal. For example, government policies in different countries come into play while analysing stocks.

In reality, when you buy shares or stocks of a company, you are buying into the security blocks of the company, which comprises the ownership. You start partially owning a company. Conversely, there are many ways of raising money through exchanges for business growth, and one of them is issuing fresh shares or bonds. There are instruments like foreign currency convertible bonds (FCCB) and global depositary receipts (GDR) that you can use towards that end. Exchanges allow flexibility of products and instruments, subject to rules and regulations.

Overall, my advice is simple. Save enough, put the money in high-yielding bonds or bank fixed deposit plans to gain interest, and invest the surplus money in stocks. Property is considered a very good alternative investment that appreciates in value.

013 | How can you avoid office politics and toxicity at work?

Politics in workplaces can be quite daunting. Sometimes, organizations become victim to employees creating power centres that lead to conflicts and manipulation. This often becomes a challenge for senior leaders. A crisis can arise when the seniors have a problem with each other or cracks develop within the board of the company.

I was quite young when I joined my father's business. The initial phase was exciting, and I was privy to the highest level of information as I was in the room where all decisions were being made, which was my father's cabin. However, when I got down to the operational level, I realized that some people in our office had a problem with others and there was frequent backbiting among colleagues. Often, my father would have to hear complaints about certain employees that influenced his decisions. I was appalled at the level of politics and realized that people sometimes refuse to see the bigger picture and just want the upper hand in the small game.

To start a company and take it to new heights, I feel that one must define the ultimate objective of the company and not allow divisive forces to creep in. An employee should be aligned with the goals of the firm and not engage in useless games that can make them a liability, divert them from achieving the company's ultimate goal and waste everyone's time. If co-workers see something like this happening, they must report it to upper management and HR professionals who can tackle the issue wisely. Office politics is best left discouraged.

A toxic work environment isn't in the best interest of any company. I would not encourage too much flexibility in work hours or unnecessary work from home, as workplaces are meant for work and homes for relaxation. Work from home is still an experiment in progress, the results of which aren't out yet.

Foul language, bad manners and lack of consideration for others are traits that make the workplace unpleasant for others, so we must do our part to make office time constructive and productive. Every day at work is a new day and a day of learning and growth. There is a lot of personal development that can happen by concentrating and being immersed in work. More importantly, while focus is important, there should be healthy colleague bonding outside of work too, a culture we now see developing everywhere.

014 | How should harness employee strength to beat sales figures?

I believe in planning and execution, and not doing things haphazardly. The government of India is known to have relied upon the concept of five-year plans, wherein a path is charted out for the next five years and the resultant plans are executed during that period. Similarly, I believe in setting targets, achieving them before time and then planning for the future. This way, growth becomes organic, systematic and satisfactory.

Companies often set marketing and sales targets for their products and services that are shared with employees who then work towards meeting them. Often, incentives are given to those who beat the numbers. A performance bonus is also a great idea. There is no harm in challenging yourself and your organization to reach higher targets, as long as they are realistic and within reach.

This method of setting periodic goals is a good way to reach the top, but it requires the full-time focus of the team. Only a good team can make leaps of progress. This method of organizational growth is safe and methodical and yields results.

015| How do you make money work for you?

Earning money isn't easy. However, if you have initial capital that you can invest as you like, making more money becomes easier. The more cash you reserve, the easier it becomes to make money work for you. Obviously, with money, you can buy many things – a car, a house, good clothes – but these are basic. How do you make money actually work for you to get even bigger and better rewards?

One of the things you could do is invest in stocks and mutual funds. Mutual funds are relatively safer than the stock market as they spread the risk across many companies instead of just one. Specialists analyse safe bets and then invest on your behalf. These days, mutual funds are very common, and I am a first-hand observer of the Indian diaspora, where these products have become very popular. Television ads and disclaimers talk about mutual funds being 'subject to market risk'. However, they are relatively safe if you go with the right products and the right company that creates the portfolios.

If you want to invest directly into the stock market, you should analyse everything from a long-term perspective and place your bets safely. You shouldn't go with quick buck tips. Instead, be safe and go with the blue-chip companies, that too after careful analysis, and create a diverse portfolio of safe options.

Investing in property is considered one of the safest

options. I asked one of the leading investors of India for his advice for some personal money that I wanted to invest, and he said that he had made money in the stock market but not everyone does and that I should definitely place it safely by buying some property. I deliberated over his advice seriously. I realized that the fall in property prices is not as much as in the stock market, which mitigates the risk. Property prices usually go up over time. There are also alternative investment funds (AIF) that are among the newer products being offered. If you are strapped for cash, you can always choose to invest through systematic investment plans (SIP).

I have never been a fan of putting capital in start-ups or new ventures, as I feel that they are too risky and too many of them fail. However, if you have money left over after the earlier-mentioned investments, you could allocate a small percentage to a start-up or venture capital fund or even a private equity (PE) fund. Better yet, start your own venture. Start small and make it grow slowly. This is of course only if you are a high-net-worth individual and want to take bets, some safe and some risky. Whatever you do, let me tell you, it is a good feeling seeing money grow, not shrink.

Lastly, you must give back to society, and you could do that in any small way. Many global NGOs accept small donations and have websites that you could use to make a difference in someone's life, as per your capacity. You could even sponsor a child's education through some of these NGO websites. Having done so myself in the past, I highly recommend doing something similar at least once in your. I sponsored a kid from Kenya and received periodical cards and thank you notes from him. Over time I did lose touch with him, and I wonder how he is now.

Give back to your college, as your college affiliation stays with you all your life. Making a contribution to your alma mater and getting others to do so as well makes a huge difference. A lot of universities depend on grants to ameliorate lives. Hence, with money, there are endless options in front of you, and how to make it work for you depends on what interests you. Some people buy yachts, planes, holiday homes and cars with their cash, which is fine too, but just don't let luxury blind you. Look at the problems of the world, and try to make a difference.

016| Why is sustainability important?

Sustainability is doing things in a way that is in the interest of the planet in the long run. Ensuring that any damage done to nature or society through our activities is remedied and working towards making our planetary impact net positive is the essence of sustainability.

You can cut down your carbon footprint, generate as little toxic waste as possible or process it before dumping it in designated places. Planting more trees also helps in making areas more environmentally sustainable. Supply chains across industries need to be altered suitably in order to produce sustainable items. Efforts should also be applied to avoid soil contamination and replenish our natural resources.

Corporate social responsibility (CSR) is a common business model employed by companies to take better account of their sustainability. It is also known as 'corporate conscience'. To make any business succeed, it is as important for society to be made a major stakeholder as it is to give back to the same society. CSR is an umbrella term that constitutes a wide range of social activities which a corporation – or a group thereof – contributes to from its profits. In some countries, it is mandatory to budget a minimum amount for CSR activities (usually a small percentage of profits).

Essentially, CSR is a glorified term for social service or philanthropy. It could be undertaken in any field and basically implies a corporation's responsibility towards society. For example, for enterprises engaged in the procurement of natural resources, CSR could involve doing things for the environment. Companies could also donate funds to NGOs working in respective fields or even start initiatives such as providing children with education, healthcare, higher education or shelter homes.

CSR could be a good opportunity to showcase the good intentions of a company and highlight its shared values with others. Some groups or companies set up foundations, just as we at Enso have, and take up work to uplift society.

For those who want to market their companies as being charitable, CSR can be the answer. It gives you a green image; in fact, it may just inspire others to follow suit. Doing good things could be a balm to your soul as well.

017 | How does a region get famous for a particular product or service?

For someone to do well in a field, expertise is essential. In today's age of globalization and laser-fast communication, people have to really know what they are doing and talking about.

Let's take the example of Germany. The country is tremendously industrialized, with one of the best technologies in heavy industries and electronic products. It is famous for its automobile industry, and three of the best automobile companies – BMW, Audi and Mercedes – are based there. In college, I remember reading a case study on how industrial know-how of the automobile industry has grown, circulated and re-evolved over generations in Germany which leads them to manufacture products of such high quality. The inner circles of these companies are constantly discussing and thinking about quality, thus refining their technical knowledge. Secrets are shared, and people learn from each other and their own mistakes over time. It's a melting-pot and think tank for industry know-how.

Another example of this is the fashion in Paris or Milan. I don't know anything about fashion, and my knowledge is constrained to what I wear and what is available off the rack. However, I do know that designers from all over the world keep an eye out for the latest trends, which come from Paris or Milan. The secret behind these European trendsetters is their deep study of the evolution of design and their own experiences in business and the world. Some of the best apparel brands that I know of are French or Italian.

Switzerland is known for its chocolates and watches; Silicon Valley in the USA for tech; New York for investment banking and consultancy; the Middle East for oil and gas; and India for IT and hospitality. Saudi Arabians know about oil and gas like experienced farmers know their farming, as it comes naturally to them. Holding these leading positions in the world markets depends on tricks of the trade, which can't be learnt overnight.

Specialization is crucial, but corporatization is a must to monetize one's advantage. Hence, while an edge definitely counts, even specialized companies have to strategize, list and raise funds to expand markets, organize and publicize in order to grow their business and brands. They also have to step a little out of their comfort zone and add to their product lines to compete with other rival brands. Chanel, Louis Vuitton, Cartier, Canali, etc., are all examples of companies constantly expanding their range of products that have reached almost all parts of the world now. We are currently living in a beautiful age of globalization, where it is possible for the best products can reach the best markets and where, from a consumer point of view, everything is easy to obtain.

OUR WORLD

018 | What are the biggest challenges facing mankind?

The biggest problem currently facing our planet is that of overpopulation and hunger, given the world population of approximately 7.7 billion. With the world's populace increasing at a rate of 1.09 per cent per year (as per data from 2018), food would eventually run out. The good news is that while the global population is still increasing, its rate peaked decades ago and as per the ongoing trend, it shall continue to decline over the next several years. However, agriculture and dairy production will have to be stepped up gradually to meet the rising demands. Prices of fishery and poultry products will inevitably go up, making it more difficult for some to obtain daily meals. Malnourishment is already a serious ongoing issue, which leads to the death of many infants in various parts of the world.

The second biggest challenge facing humanity is poverty. People lose their homes and are forced to sleep on the streets, despite serious illnesses and injuries. It is sadly a common sight in the developing economies of African nations, India, Bangladesh and Pakistan to see homeless, sometimes even physically challenged, individuals to beg on the roads. Whenever possible, I like to offer monetary help, in the hope that they are able to do better and afford food and other basic resources. There, however, is a dire need for an organized effort, at the national level, to help rehabilitate the poor and make them a part of mainstream economy. Poverty should be looked at as an opportunity to improve rather than a liability.

Poverty almost always leads to crime and, thus, the entire ecosystem gets maligned. The solution would be to encourage businesses, for example in the agricultural sector, where employment can be readily generated. People stepping up to build shelters for the homeless could also work as an effective solution. Economies have to prosper in order for the last person in the chain to be affected positively. CSR and philanthropic efforts can also be stepped up in this direction.

The third challenge facing humanity is the state of basic healthcare and general health awareness. Right from proper vaccinations for infants to daily health directives, the third world economies need the world's urgent attention and action. For this, good governance is the only hope. Health awareness needs to reach every single person across land borders. When we talk of poverty, we only think of the financially poor, but what of the tribals in the remote areas of India and countries in Africa? With close to no access to electricity, medical supplies, clean water, toilets, banking, internet or mobile network, more often than not basic amenities don't even reach them. One drought can lead to death by starvation. In these regions, resources need to be pooled and made accessible.

Mental health conditions today are more and more prevalent. We cannot fathom what an impediment a condition like depression or bipolar disorder becomes. It could be a lifelong struggle. To avoid such mental health related-issues, resources should be made available for people to live naturally and avoid stress. Healthy habits and simplicity of life could prove to be alleviating.

Covid-19 was a recent force majeure and highlighted all that can go wrong in a blink. While we should feel fortunate that global economies were not completely shaken, we should draw lessons of humanity and solidarity from this past saga, and move forward in a more prepared manner, lest something like this happen again.

The fourth challenge facing the world is illiteracy. Children should be taught how to read and write. But how can they, when they are faced with extreme circumstances wherein parents have to make the hard decision between providing their children basic education or inducting them to work on farms or getting menial jobs to make ends meet? To reiterate, awareness and opportunities are essential.

I sponsored a few children in Tanzania through World Vision and received handwritten letters from them. I was all smiles that day, and it gave me immense joy to have done something meaningful. We should seriously spare a thought for our global community. My family lives in Mumbai, and we have the luxury of employing house help and drivers. Some of them are fortunate to afford proper education for their children, while some others struggle to get from one day to the next given the high costs of living in a big city. This really saddens me. If we move forward, even slow and steady, progress can be made. Girl child education needs to be promoted even more passionately.

The fifth major challenge facing mankind is the deteriorating state of nature. Even though the greenhouse effect and climate change are taking a toll on our planet, the intelligent go-green drive is trying to make life better for everyone and giving us hope in the midst of a critical situation. We are seeing the rise of dependence on solar, tidal, wind and nuclear energy, which are all renewable and environmentally friendly. This development needs to be stepped up as, with time, renewable sources can be harnessed cheaply and for as long as we want, while hydrocarbons in all their forms are limited. Pollution of land, water and the air is causing ailments among humans and other species. Life-threatening illnesses like cancer are on the rise. Oceans are getting affected and thereby, due to contamination, marine life suffers. Plastic waste disposal is toxic to the soil and water and doesn't disintegrate for decades, if not centuries.

There are many other issues facing the world today, such as gender inequality, terrorism and the moral downgrade of society, which I have touched upon in other essays in this book. The opportunities of our world are becoming better than ever before, but we need to step up efforts to make it greener, cleaner and more equal for all.

019| Why is world peace important?

Atomic bombing has been witnessed twice, at Hiroshima and Nagasaki in Japan at the end of World War II, and history still speaks of those dark days. Luckily, we haven't seen this happen again since. Nevertheless, nations have long been in the race to be the superior military power. Why so? If you ask me, economic superiority is way more important than that, as is the happiness index of its people. According to me, ease of doing business in a country deserves more attention than the number of nuclear warheads it possesses.

In 2017, the Nobel Peace Prize was awarded to the International Campaign to Abolish Nuclear Weapons (ICAN). ICAN was launched in 2007 and, as of 2017, counts 468 partner organizations in 101 countries. The conferment reiterated the importance of world peace.

Most countries of the world adhere to the Nuclear Non-Proliferation Treaty (NPT), except India, Israel and Pakistan. The USA and Russia have the highest number of munition, followed by the UK, France and China. India and Pakistan have warheads in the range of 100–150 each. North Korea and Israel have also developed some nukes, but due to neutralization, have stopped further work. Each missile has the capacity to take down a major portion of a fully flourishing megacity. But why possess such weapons? If no one has them, there will be no race for this potentially destructive investment!

I feel that if disarmament is not in the pipeline, each nation should stop further work, come clean about their arsenal and divert the funds towards health, education and other constructive things. The only use I see for these bombs is in case of a major asteroid threat. There still isn't strong evidence suggesting the existence of aliens. So if human beings design weapons to kill other humans, the window of hope will only get narrower and narrower. If one ghastly day, someone uses these weapons, we will fall back by years in history and witness unimaginable unrest. Everyone will feel unsafe for years to come, and the consequence could be highly destructive wars. Nuclear non-proliferation is the way to go.

The recent looming threat of World War III began with four conflicts: Russia's war against Ukraine, Taiwan being backed by the USA against China, India locked between Pakistan and China and the Israel–Palestine war. The situation is still precarious, and anything can happen. Every time things escalate to a high degree, pacifists beg for peace. Stock markets come crashing down. So clearly, geopolitics and Covid-19 have changed the world a lot.

020 | What is the difference between citizenship and nationality?

How I see it, a country or a state is a sovereign entity with geographical boundaries, while a nation is a group of people united by a common culture, pledging allegiance to a particular country, that may or may not be the one they reside in. So, while a country is a legal entity, a nation is not. For example, Indians born in India but living in England carry British passports and belong to the UK, but they may pledge allegiance to India during a cricket match between India and England. Thus, they are of Indian origin, which is their nationality, but doesn't define their citizenship. A citizen of a country holds the passport of that country. These days, some countries even allow dual citizenship.

We often see Indian Prime Minister Narendra Modi getting huge cheers among overseas crowds of Indian nationality. These people may be citizens of different countries, but they or their families are mostly of Indian origin, which gives them an Indian nationality. The idea of India binds them together. Countries acknowledge that, and these people are given a Person of Indian Origin (PIO) or an Overseas Citizen of India (OCI) status and an OCI card for easy travel to and from India.

To make this distinction clearer, India only become a 'country' once it attained its independence from British rule.

A nation, too, is a strong identity and cannot be ignored. In my view, it's an ideology and a fraternity that can welcome almost anybody. You can choose your citizenship, even though incumbents tend to be sentimental about it. People of Indian origin living in different parts of the world still belong to the Indian nation as they preserve and maintain their culture, salute their flag, follow the developments of their ancestral homeland and smile at every achievement of India. I strongly feel that, while sometimes people take up a different citizenship, they ought to consider not letting go of their places of origin.

The other citizens in a new country one is emigrating to may not be as accepting of someone of a different culture or skin colour, but there are economic benefits or career amelioration opportunities that may be more attractive in a foreign land. In such a situation, people often have to evolve and integrate into the foreign society. Luckily for us, India has a great pacifist reputation overseas, and people of Indian origin don't have to struggle that much. People from some countries have it much harder owing to their country's dubious geopolitical involvements.

Among high achievers from India doing well overseas are Satya Nadella who is leading Microsoft, Indra Nooyi who led Pepsico, Subra Suresh who was president of Carnegie Mellon University, Sundar Pichai who is leading Google, Bobby Jindal who was the 55th Governor of Louisiana state in the US, Nitin Nohria who was the dean of Harvard Business School followed by Srikant Dattar, Soumitra Dutta who is the dean of Said Business School at the University of Oxford, Shantanu Narayen who is the CEO of Adobe, the former CEO of Twitter, Parag Agrawal and so on. The list is long. Kamala Harris, the Vice President of the USA and Rishi

Sunak, the Prime Minister of the UK, are leading sovereign states and their prenatal link to India signifies acceptance of the Indian nationality by the larger community in major economies.

While the distinction between nation and country is from political science, I thought it was important to touch upon as so many people don't know the difference, even when it's directly relevant to them, especially with the amount of migration happening. India's brain drain can be a brain gain in the long run if OCIs and NRIs start contributing back to India and its economy or repatriate. For that, there has to be a level playing field in India for start-ups, and the ecosystem has to be improved, especially in terms of the ease of doing business.

Niccolo Machiavelli defines patriotism as 'the love of common liberty that enabled citizens to see their private and particular interest as part of the common good'. That is, in a conservative sense, a great definition. Patriotism could be towards multiple nations, as we see in the case of migrants and foreign returns.

021 | Are hydrocarbons ever going to be required in the future?

Our dependency should shift from oil to gas-based fuels, for they are cleaner forms of energy and lead to fewer and/or less toxic emissions. We live at a time when the rush for oil is continuing to take over the world, affecting the political alignment of nations and businesses and even causing wars. Businesses and nations are rushing after precious hydrocarbons. Prices of oil are still usually controlled by the Middle East-led cartel called Organization of the Petroleum Exporting Countries (OPEC), and most countries in the world consider them as being pivotal for their survival.

At the same time, greater awareness about climate change and the greenhouse effect has led people to invest more money in research on renewable sources of energy, such as solar, wind, tidal, biomass and nuclear. I strongly believe that a greener planet is in the interest of our future generations, and this revolution is in the right direction.

Vehicles are becoming electric, and we are heading towards a time when almost the entire planet's energy needs are met by these renewable sources of energy. Consequently, of course, oil needs are slowly but surely reducing. Thus, we see that oil-based economies are now developing alternative sources of income. Oil and gas, no doubt, are precious commodities. The fossil fuel reserves on the planet need the world's urgent attention as they continue depleting. The prices of oil and gas keep rising even as our dependence on them lessens.

I must add here that renewable energy is cheaper and more sustainable than hydrocarbon-based energy production. The dependence of oil and gas on petrochemicals and other such products will not vanish in the near future, and neither will OPEC's control of the prices of oil and gas. Russia has shown that it is a mighty power when it comes to the supply of oil and gas, and has one of the largest reserves of natural gas in the world. That is a fact that has become abundantly clear from the Russia–Ukraine war of 2022.

Overall, dependency on hydrocarbons will decrease owing to a paradigm shift towards green and renewable sources of energy. My guesstimate is that the Paris Agreement, combined with the sustainability revolution, will see us through to cleaner energy sources. To the best of my knowledge, nuclear power holds the key to the future, simply because of the sheer scale at which it generates power.

Coal-based power plants are being shut down and facing heavy fines, as they are carbon unfriendly and people want to do away with pollutants. The shift is towards nuclear power with hydrogen backing solar, wind and tidal power.

Most of these sources are being subsidized in India. India has set a target of 2070 for net zero emissions. I think we can get there earlier, as the pace of transition is going to pick up. Globally, the Paris Agreement's aim of strengthening the world's response to the threat of climate change is a strong step in the right direction. The goal is to 'keep global temperature rise this century below 2 degrees Celsius above pre-industrial levels and to pursue efforts to limit the temperature increase even further to 1.5 degrees Celsius'.

022 | Isn't GDP per capita a more apt measure of prosperity than GDP?

While the scale for the development of any country is measured by its GDP – the aggregate of goods and services produced by the country – it is definitely not enough to measure this figure in isolation and use it to determine a country's wealth.

Measuring the income level of the population spread and how much each person earns is important and can often be a better measure of how well an economy is doing. It is very obvious that the bigger the population, the more hands working towards growing a nation.

It is very easy to publish GDP figures and GDP growth rate, but one must also take a look at GDP per capita, as that shows the sum total of wealth of a country's production; it indicates the strength of the participants of the economy – its working population.

The USA's population is close to 220 million, and its GDP is close to USD 20 trillion. On the other hand, India's population is approximately 1.3 billion, and its GDP is close to USD 3 trillion. The contrast is sharp, but this number is not enough. Simply being in the top ten economies of the world in terms of GDP doesn't indicate prosperity. One must take into account the country's population as well. India ranks in the top 100 on the list of GDP per capita, which is at approximately USD 2,000, while the USA is in the top 10, with a whopping figure of around USD 60,000

023| Is brain drain ever good?

With a population of around 7.7 billion, the world is fast becoming densely populated. However, we must bear in mind that it's not a problem if resources are appropriately allocated to nurture human potential.

Many countries like Russia, Canada, Australia and certain possess vast tracts of uninhabited land, including desert nations like Saudi Arabia and more. I love the idea of a human resource industry where skilled labour migrates from densely populated regions to such sparsely populated ones. This approach not only addresses the demand for skilled workers but also leads to economic balance, often resulting in higher earnings for the workers themselves. A unified world can make this transformation of population adjustment possible. Countries like Canada actively encourage people to come and work there. This is where demand meets supply.

In India's context, this movement of workers is a double-edged sword. While we have a substantial number of unemployed people who can greatly benefit from employment abroad, we are aware that our best minds choose to leave the country This brain drain isn't in the interest of our country. To attract these individuals we have to work on making India a level playing field, free of corruption and bureaucracy. We also have to make India safer to increase the number of foreign students, which currently stands at a remarkably low figure of 75,000 per year. Our public safety standards as well as civic amenities need to be upgraded to attract and retain talent.

024 | Why should the Gini coefficient be monitored around the world?

The Gini coefficient is a ratio between 0 and 1 that measures the divide between the rich and the poor in an economy. A value of 0 means that income is evenly divided, while 1 means that one person holds all the wealth of the country. The top 1 per cent of the population of wage earners in the US have average earnings of around USD 718,766, which comprises a 13.4 per cent share of all wages in the country. The top 5 per cent are placed at around USD 299,810, and they make about 28.1 per cent of all wages. The top 10 per cent average at USD 118,400 per annum. Others make significantly less money. This sample data shows that immense income disparity among the top 10 per cent, but what is startling is the drastic difference lower down the scale. The fall is a landslide, evident in a large enough sample, within the most powerful and robust economy, ranking highest in terms of GDP and within the top 10 in GDP per capita. The Gini coefficient of the USA is around 0.5. Just imagine the disparity in poorer countries.

The world's billionaires, who account for a small fraction of the global population, have amassed massive fortunes. In the 32nd annual Forbes list of the world's billionaires, the aggregate wealth of the top 20 richest people on Earth amounts to about 13 percent of all billionaires' fortunes combined. 'A record of 2,208 billionaires were in the ranking and the total wealth was $9.1 trillion, up 18%,' said a Google search during the pandemic in 2020. These figures are surprising and give an indication as to what those at the top ought to do to uplift those at the bottom. The top 0.1 per cent of the world's population makes more than the bottom 90 per cent. That is a vast gap.

In the last decade and a half many countries have made strides to uplift the poor and integrate them with the middle class. The availability of statistics, facts and figures has helped governments crunch data faster, thus enabling them to identify what jobs can be created and where. A measure of success for any country now hinges not only on their GDP growth but also on lowering their unemployment level.

As wealth trickles down and reaches the people who are in dire need, we see that it helps people at the top make more money, as these people can now afford industrial products and become consumers, thus buying into the businesses of the rich. A financially sound populace is in the interest of every stakeholder in the country's growth. Bridging the gap between the rich and poor is important and should be at the forefront of every government mandate.

025 | What are the consequences of letting terrorism breed?

When the 9/11 attacks happened, I was in eleventh grade. A group of us had plans to travel to Boston to attend the Harvard Model United Nations (HMUN). Suddenly, things turned scary, and our parents began deliberating whether we should go or not. Fortunately, they decided that we should go, and so we did. Much to our dismay, we saw how security at the airports had been amped up, and the immigration officers in Newark airport were being awfully rude to foreigners. People were alarmed at what was happening.

This was in 2001. A couple of years later in 2003, I went to Pittsburgh to attend college at Carnegie Mellon. The situation had still not settled, with everyone tense and on edge. Foreigners like me underwent extensive scanning at airport security, and there were all sorts of precautionary measures that homeland security and the police implemented across the country to prevent anything similar from happening again.

For years, Afghanistan remained a war zone, and it's unfortunate for the innocent locals there who had to suffer and witness death and destruction for years. For all we know, behind Osama Bin Laden's religious fanaticism could well be a desire to be famous, which led him to execute such a major attack, killing innocents and destroying the fabric of New York, which took a long time to repair.

Similarly, attacks occurred in Mumbai on 26 November 2011. These were carried out by Pakistani extremists whose sole agenda was to rampantly kill innocents and weaken the morale of India. With their actions, they succeeded in curbing the freedom of Indians across all cities. Every hotel in the country has security checkpoints, not one, but two – one for vehicles and another for people. For a long time, foreigners probably thought twice before coming to India as the venues targeted were those visited most by tourists – hotels and restaurants. The attacks were carefully planned and designed to deter foreigners from visiting India's financial capital.

More recently, Europe has experienced many assaults by individuals influenced by ISIS and its ideologies. This is deeply unsettling and people live in fear – the reaction terrorists want. In many instances, they don't care about their own lives. If the sense of unity of the people gets stronger, the terrorists are weakened. That is why we must be brave and optimistic, believing that all this will end one day.

What is it that makes people do these dastardly things? The answer isn't clear to me. If it's religion, they definitely don't know what God is. If it's personal fame, they should know that they will be on the run for the rest of their lives, and it isn't a worthwhile trade-off, as more often than not, they will be caught or killed. If it's money that they are after, they should understand that once they are apprehended, that money will just be used for their coffins and graves. Let's hope better sense prevails and people employ their religious freedom to better their lives, earn an honourable living and coexist peacefully while letting others to live in peace as well.

Terrorists are indeed cowards, targetting innocent and unprepared people. But because of them, others are forced to live in constant fear. In India, hotels and airports are carefully guarded till date, and what used to be an open walk-in is now interrupted with multiple security checks. As responsible citizens, we have to be vigilant and fight any inkling of these activities, no matter what part of the world we reside in.

Countries are laying emphasis on strengthening Interpol as a global body to capture and punish criminals. This will make it harder for any perpetrator to escape.

026| Are wars sometimes necessary?

No one likes wars. They cause destruction and lead to casualties and throw nations back by years. In the last two decades, we witnessed terrible wars where alliances led by the USA and the UK, primarily the North Atlantic Treaty Organization (NATO), uprooted the ruthless rulers of the Middle East. Saddam Hussein of Iraq and his son were killed, and effective democracy was installed in the country. Similarly, terrible atrocities were committed by the former ruler of Libya, Gaddafi, who was prosecuted to make way for human rights in the country. Syria remained a battleground as the country saw the rise of ISIS on its soil, as Russia, under Vladimir Putin's rule, volunteered to get rid of the miscreants. Assad compromised and volunteered to be a just ruler. Wars were also fought in Egypt and Yemen. Hosni Mubarak succumbed to the people of Egypt when they revolted against him and went to jail. Late George Bush Sr. had forced a Kuwaiti ruler to step down as Afghanistan's head of state during his presidency. There has been mayhem, no doubt, but these were necessary actions. More recently, Ashraf Ghani's office was abolished as the Taliban took over the country.

Many of these countries were ruled by some families for generations, and the rulers were so drunk with power that they not only troubled locals – often raping, plundering and killing mercilessly – but they also threatened other nations, as per media reports.

I have been part of the oil and gas industry long enough to confirm that these wars were started by nations that were genuinely concerned. They were not fought for access to oil and gas resources in that land. Instead, they were driven by concern for the people of these countries and to maintain human rights. The USA, under Barack Obama, along with a strong NATO alliance, fought against what seemed like demonic forces.

I know a lady who was under house arrest in Libya for years before NATO forces freed her. The atmosphere in these lands was that of perpetual fear and lawlessness. Nobody could imagine human rights and justice ever coming to get them. These wars were expensive, with trillions of dollars spent on them, and yet they were necessary. This amount cannot be recovered even by taking over these nations' hydrocarbons and other resources for some time in the future.

The locals of these countries never experienced hope under the earlier regimes, but now they do. The decimation of life and property and the long list of martyrs is a heavy price mankind has had to pay for these wars of justice, but if these steps hadn't been taken, the people residing in these nations would never know what freedom is, and they would never get equal and fair opportunities.

Redevelopment work is the obvious next step. I am very happy that more countries in the region are stepping up to lend a hand to their less fortunate neighbours. Saudi Arabia has committed to taking care of Syria. Similarly, India and other nations are helping Afghanistan. Former leaders Barack Obama and David Cameron have done a lot of good work in this direction, and it is the responsibility of their successors to restore these economies. A country that destroys the property of another in a war needs to reimburse them for the reconstruction as per international laws that define conflict situations. However, that is not enough in this case. The world must go the extra mile to build, rebuild, repair and heal.

027| What is China doing wrong?

China has long been studied for its meteoric rise in terms of economic and GDP growth. It has done extremely well in terms of infrastructure growth and urban development, so much so that it has now become a focal point as an industrial centre for global companies to set up shop, given the availability of skilled and low-wage labour. Other overhead costs are low too, and tremendous incentives are given to the industrial sector. Chinese leaders should feel proud of their accomplishments, because this progress is excellent. Chinese universities rank fairly high globally too and the country is gaining ground in the field of innovations and disruptions, something their nearby archipelago nation, Japan, has always been known for.

There are some things that, I would say, are deterrents for China to reach the pinnacle of success. While their growth has been exponential, they still don't adhere to net neutrality. Many foreign tech companies, such as Twitter and Facebook, have been denied entry into China. Google has been denied full freedom, and thus their market penetration has been limited. Being a communist nation, its people have very little say in matters of governance. The media, too, isn't known to be very powerful in China.

China's Communist Party is the second largest party in the world after India's Bharatiya Janata Party (BJP). There have been reports of media oppression, corruption and restricted access to the outside world through the internet at the hands of the party. This is a huge negative point for the Chinese, as people-to-people interaction with the world beyond their boundaries is limited and the information they obtain about the outside world is heavily restricted. I hope that there is a dawn of e-experiences for the vast majority of the population that craves for it. They should also come clean with human rights violation allegations by letting the media do its job.

China is a fabulous model for growth, one people envy and look up to. However, sacrificing the happiness of the people for the sake of economic growth is a huge, coercive price to pay for it. Today, people aim to be global citizens, and there are aspirations of a unified world that transcends all boundaries. Why curtail that?

028| What is India's business forte?

India obtained independence on 15 August 1947, and since then the government has worked hard to improve the economy and struggled to balance a large population living in poverty, striving to meet their daily requirements, while also meeting the expectations of the affluent, who desire world-class development in the country. There has always been a significant gap between the rich and the poor in India, posing a persistent challenge for every government.

Corruption in India has been rampant, right from the top to the very bottom. This culture has become a curse for the land, but luckily, a lot is being done to address this issue. The top is clearing out slowly, but the bottom and middle tiers of bureaucracy will take some time. However, there is progress.

Family businesses have prospered in our country, but sadly, that is owing to crony capitalism, especially in the past. Sometimes, access is the only thing that counts, and that is why business houses have lasted generations in our land. Budding entrepreneurs have had to develop connections to actually understand how the system functions.

India's license raj, or the tender system, for obtaining licenses to operate various businesses, has frequently been exploited by unscrupulously rigging the specifications for the high and mighty, who exploit their cash power. This has resulted in slow progress as the right candidates often don't get a fair chance, while incumbents might be slow in execution or lacking quality. However, this is slowly coming to an end and the exchequer is strong today. Anyone can file a Right to Information (RTI) query, which could then lead to a public interest litigation (PIL). The media too keeps a strong check on corruption.

According to me, a new wave of liberalization is required to tackle this problem, and power has to go back to the people, who should not require so many government permits to operate. De-regulation can be amazing for the economy.

India has seen a wave of technology start-ups, right from websites to mobile apps. Bengaluru, the tech capital of India, has seen recent investments from all corners of the world, leading to the emergence of many new unicorn startups. Quality services are starting to make life easier for the people of India. Right from online payments to farmers wanting goods delivered to their doorsteps, there are now websites and mobile applications providing these services. FinTech is getting smoother and more secure.

Information technology, owing to India's incumbency in the software industry, is doing very well globally, and we have various new additions to the largest firms – Tata Consultancy Services (TCS), Infosys, Mahindra Satyam. Due to the cheap and skilled workforce available in India, business process outsourcing (or BPO), such as call centres and back-end working of large global companies, is being done in the country. This is a huge cost cut for the companies and an employment generator for India. The textile industry is huge in India, as foreign brands often outsource manufacturing to Indian manufacturers. Another beautiful industry that India prides itself on is the hospitality industry. We have great hotels and resorts, and tourists from the world over come to vacation here as we have the right mix of history, beaches and mountains, combined with a welcoming attitude.

Today, India has made considerable advances in the field of telecom services. Even though the nation imports large amounts of oil to meet its current demands, India has one of the largest refineries in the world. The oil and gas industry is expanding, with the continuing production of petroleum products and exploration for further reserves. India conducts mineral and metal mining activities and has a high steel output, which caters to local needs and accounts for a large percentage of export. India is self-sufficient in the pharmaceutical industry and doing well in many more sectors, thanks to government support, periodical policy improvements, international tie-ups and ambitious businessmen driving robust economic growth.

I believe India needs to focus on quality research and development (R&D) along with technological tie-ups to take the lead in some industries and create its own disruptions. Universities in India need to step up and contribute to nurturing world-class professionals. Currently, there are only a handful and thus we lag behind in innovation and are still an offshoring destination.

029| What exactly is the Kashmir dispute?

India and Pakistan were one country until a recent point in history. The two regions were united within the Indian subcontinent until the later stages of British colonial rule. Under the leadership of Mohammed Ali Jinnah, a movement emerged for the creation of Pakistan; imagined as a nation where Muslims could live without external influence. While Pakistan gained independence on 14 August 1947, India was born one day later. While they had been one land for centuries, discord between the two nations led to communal riots, and many Hindus and Muslims were mercilessly killed. The aftermath was the start of an issue that lingers even today – the control of Kashmir. The belief, held by many, of this northernmost state being an integral part of India, has been contested by Pakistan, which maintains that the people of Kashmir, primarily Muslims, want to become a part of Pakistan.

Many Indians blame Jawaharlal Nehru, India's first prime minister, for letting it be a princely state and not taking over Kashmir with the help of the army when it was possible. He had instead chosen to take the dispute to the United Nations in 1948. The border dispute has now been pending for over seven decades, with no solution in sight.

In 1971, a war between India and Pakistan broke out, which resulted in the formation of Bangladesh from 'East

Pakistan' with India's support. Skirmishes took place at the Indo–Pak border of Kashmir. On 3 July 1972, the Simla Agreement was signed between India and Pakistan, calling for a ceasefire and the establishment of a Line of Control (LoC) in Jammu and Kashmir, which remains enforced to this day.

India has been at the receiving end of terrorism, allegedly by the ISI, Pakistan's intelligence agency, and has taken a strong stance against its neighbour's efforts. The Kashmir issue has now received global attention. As a result, Pakistan has been on the receiving end of some terrible publicity. I hope the issue is resolved soon. There are many outfits in Kashmir that want it to be an independent country. However, I personally don't see that as a possibility.

On a slightly different note, Jammu and Kashmir is extremely scenic, being home to a part of the Himalayan range, and the tourism industry continues to develop. But the persistent political tensions and safety issues form a barrier to this growth. China usurped a large part of this territory in 1965, which is still under their administration. The land beyond the Line of Actual Control (LAC) is called Aksai Chin and remains disputed. Pakistan-occupied Kashmir (PoK) is also disputed land. Thus, Kashmir is currently divided into three parts.

The Indian government recently abrogated Article 370, which revoked Jammu and Kashmir's special status and instead turned it into a union territory (UT) of India.

I visited Leh–Ladakh a few years ago. The army movements there made me feel like I was in a war zone. Let's hope this issue sees a resolution soon and we, along with international tourists, can visit Jammu and Kashmir from both Pakistan and India's side. 'Love thy neighbour' could still be a truism, and the day cross-border tourism and trade take an upturn for good, we will know a resolution is reached, either officially or in the hearts of the people on both sides of the LoC.

030 | Has religious bigotry in India reached the point of communal tensions?

India is a secular country where citizens of all religions hold equal rights. The majority of Indians are Hindus, and in minority are people from many other religions – Muslims, Christians, Zoroastrians, Jains, Buddhists and Jews. I find this to be an interesting mix. I strongly believe that religion should be rooted in personal belief and am personally against its institutionalization.

Let me explain my view of the situation in India by citing an example. Back in the sixteenth century, the Mughal ruler Babar built a mosque in Ayodhya in the state of Uttar Pradesh – a land considered sacred by the Hindus for its mythological links to Lord Ram. Fast-forward to the late twentieth century, some thirty years ago, an angry mob broke down this mosque. There were riots all over the country. Many lost their lives, and the resultant court case lasted for years. The Hindus wanted the land to build a Ram temple, while the Muslims wanted justice for the demolition and asked to retain the land.

Left up to me, I would have just let the land be and built a national monument to display India's religious diversity that people could visit. The entire thing is preposterous. If people on both sides knew the true meaning of religious faith, they would come forward with grace and volunteer their surrender.

Thus, we see that faith has become a matter of ego and pride in the country. The Babri Masjid issue would have been resolved much faster and more smoothly if the people were more giving.

The Supreme Court of India ruled in favour of the Hindu claim on that land in April 2019, and a temple is being constructed on that land. A mosque will also be built nearby. Instead of making it an issue of Hindu–Muslim antagonism, the episode could have been used to nurture brotherhood.

Muslims in India often live in Muslim-dominated areas in big cities of India, in cliques they find comfort in. Some small towns and villages are Muslim-dominated. Christians and people of all other faiths are more intermixed in terms of demographics, but that is also due to socio-economic parameters. There have been stories of attacks on Christian priests and nuns, showing the religious discord and intolerance of a few bigots. Jews in India have experienced prejudice too. Such instances occur among the uneducated and underprivileged a lot more frequently.

Indians who are educated and working professionals are much more likely to see these actions as shameful. They would try to represent their faith in the best possible way and confine it to personal prayers and solace. Better informed people usually do not resort to unlawful acts to enforce their religion's superiority over others. They are also much more open to healthy debates.

Things should improve for minorities. What I don't like is that communalism seeps into election mandates, while the real issues take the back seat. People should rise above religion and see how far the world has reached and aim to take the country there.

Religious bigotry has been witnessed in many parts of the world and in various periods of history. For example, there have been attacks on synagogues in the US and more recent attacks in the UK and the rest of Europe. The 9/11 attacks had a religious angle too. Historically, the same thing can be seen in Adolf Hitler's massacre of the Jews. All of this goes to show how disconnected with their own religion these people are, and the lengths they would go just to exercise their power and show their might. They may even carry out what people now view as a crusade.

There are many examples of inter-religious unity in India too, but I am highlighting here the not-so-pleasant aspects. People of all faiths should strive towards making India a happier place for all. Everyone should practise their religion in their personal space and respect diverse views, practices, sentiments and traditions.

India is considered to be one of the most diverse nations on this planet, and we have so many socio-economic problems that the last thing we need is communal hatred. Rise up, people of India, and enrich India with 'beauty in diversity'!

According to me, Indians are overtly religious. There are also many superstitions that should be weeded out. The solution for intolerance is better education and higher income levels, which would organically replace the need to assert oneself or one's religious identity with the need for peace and tranquillity. After all, religion is supposed to provide happiness, not unrest.

031 | What has made the USA what it is today?

The USA is the largest economic and military power in the world today. The reasons for this phenomenal growth of the country are manifold. First of all, unlike other countries that attained freedom from colonial rule in the nineteenth and twentieth centuries, the USA became a free country in 1776, much earlier than any other Europe-ruled colony. Had the USA not been under colonial rule, would it have experienced greater success today? My thought process leads to the answer 'no', as these colonies brought to this disconnected land a lot of learning, experience, people, industrialization, infrastructure and evolved institutions in the field of law, education and governance. More importantly, it unified the country.

Since aeons, the USA has been a free land; free not just from colonial rule but also from the influence of the church. The fabric of religious dogma escaped this country, giving rise to unapologetic capitalism. The market for the USA's products was large, both within and outside the country's geographical confines. The government of this 'free world', I must say, ploughed back the exchequer's funds for infrastructure development – roads, railways, airports, well-planned cities – and other amenities that made the system fair and encouraged growth.

Corruption in the USA has always been under check;

even today, it is as good as non-existent. Full marks to the morals and ethics of Americans and able law enforcement. Corruption has been a huge problem in various other parts of the world, where the systems have been corroded by unfair practices. Cornelius Vanderbilt, Andrew Carnegie, David Rockefeller, J.P. Morgan and Thomas Edison were all-time greats, in business, in philanthropy and as guiding pillars for the leaders of USA. Even now, we have Bill Gates, Warren Buffet, Jeff Bezos, Mark Zuckerberg, Elon Musk and others who top the charts of the wealthy. They are also, just like their predecessors, deploying their resources to a large degree for the betterment of others.

There is something about the values of American culture that makes people benevolent to others. American culture initially evolved from European cultures, but today it has its own distinguished quality, which is reflected in its supreme position in movies and music too. The most famous brands in the world are American. One reason for this is that the USA is positioned correctly in the world as a leader and has a reputation for superior quality goods. People, globally, tend to adopt American products without a doubt about their quality.

Being the largest economy in the world has given the country enough funds for the latest warfare equipment, research in nuclear weapons, a large army and solid intelligence that can take on the best in the world. The USA has been known to maintain a no-nonsense attitude and with the help of allied forces like NATO, the country has waged wars on foreign shores for human rights issues, overthrowing dictators and establishing the people's rule. The Cold War has polarized the USA and Russia, but there is no world-threatening territorial dispute, though what lingers lingers often erupts like a volcano, as it did recently when the USA imposed sanctions on Russia as a consequence of the Russia–Ukraine war.

While we are all praises for this nation, we should talk about things that are not so perfect too – casual racism, liberal gun laws and of late, some increased xenophobia, especially in specific states.

The large landmass of the US doesn't lack natural resources either. The country boasts of surplus agricultural production and agro-based products. Overall, the country has been blessed with resources, leadership and a strong culture of free thinking, along with good climatic conditions in many regions. The American dream is a strong narrative and people are united by it. They work towards individual progress and are not satisfied with just remaining a dot in the larger scheme of things. Think of how many inventions have originated in the US in comparison to the rest of the world. The country has been disruptive in its products, a leader in terms of growth and a beacon of inspiration for all nations to follow.

032| Where is Russia on the economic map?

Russia is among the fifteen largest economies in the world and is making consistent progress. The country stretches across eleven time zones and spreads across both Europe and Asia. It is the largest country in the world by land mass. Russia has the second-largest military in the world and the largest reserve of proven natural gas resources. It is in the top ten in terms of oil reserves. Being in the northern belt and high up in latitude, the winters there are really harsh, constraining agriculture to the summertime and thus to just one crop per year. Vodka is a Russian invention, and the Russians drink a lot, especially during the winter, to stay warm.

Moscow, the capital city of Russia, is beautiful. The people are really nice, which I can tell you from first-hand experience, as I visited the country in 2013. St Petersburg is supposed to be one of the most beautiful European cities, and I definitely want to visit it, having heard a lot about it. Hailed as the 'Venice of Russia', it makes for an amazing tourist destination, and has witnessed great glory and the ruin of the Russian Czars. Sochi too is considered to be a must-visit for tourists.

Russian eggs are among the most famous of their souvenirs and are often hand painted. I proudly display one in my room. All in all, there are old and non-factual myths surrounding Russia and its business friendliness.

Led by Vladimir Putin, Russia annexed a part of northern Ukraine, Crimea, in the twenty-first century. More recently, Russia attacked Ukraine, making the threat of World War III imminent. War looming over Asian soil is no new occurrence, but Russia balances American hegemony in world geopolitics.

People have often associated Russia with the mafia and government expropriation. Both are defunct notions, as the country is extremely business-friendly today. The leaders are trying hard to bring industries into the country and grow its GDP. The eastern belt of the country, near Vladivostok, being close to the sea, is being considered as a hub for industrialization, with investments in the area being encouraged.

In my view, what the Russian government should do is clarify the rumours around the business climate by conducting interviews with their leaders in the global press and continue efforts to bring in investment for better growth and development. Another thing they could do, especially since they have so much land, is to import skilled manpower of various nationalities and focus on the settlement of quality human capital entering the country. Russia's relationship with China and India is healthy, and that is good for peace and economic stability in Asia. We all know that we would rather spend our defence budget on productive issues, and we all have a common enemy in terror groups.

Russia can look forward for economic prowess in the twenty-second century and work doggedly towards it.

033 | Is a body like the European Union sustainable?

The European Union (EU) came into existence on 1 November 1993 and has 28 member nations. Subsequent treaties have brought these countries closer for trade and development, encouraging the free flow of people, goods, services and finances. The EU has been an answer to the American economic monopoly and often acts as one entity. Today, all of the EU's members follow one currency, the Euro, and one visa, Schengen. In 2016, through a nationwide referendum, Britan voted out of the EU in a move that was termed Brexit.

I feel the model of the EU is amazing in terms of viewing the future of all countries across the globe in a similar manner – standing united as one, having a common currency and supporting each other through thick and thin. Its Latin motto, 'In Varietate Concordia', means 'United in Diversity', highlighting the varied cultures of the European nations. Member states of the EU have different languages and histories. However, laws on subjects in which the member states are bound together have been made uniform.

Although the geographical size of European countries is not large, they have seen colonial glory in the past and remain among the top few economies of the world, particularly Germany, Britain and France which rank within the top 10 globally. The combined GDP of the EU is somewhat close to that of USA.

I am a critic of the way Schengen countries issue short-term visas, which I feel is a deterrent to doing business and inviting tourism. They should recognize the hassle in obtaining visas and consider that issuing visas valid for five or ten years would be in their long-term interest.

What countries are doing under the EU is what should happen globally – a common currency, internal visa-free travel, common laws wherever possible, and, in addition to all this, a common legal language – English. This is my version of the 'One World' dream, which is far from being a reality today. But who knows what the future holds? It might just come true, bringing the world closer and closer to becoming one.

The EU is an amazing body and celebrates diversity in a beautiful way. It has sought to find practical solutions to counter the global economic dominance of other nations and united for effective competition. All in all, full marks to this establishment that weaves Europe into a single fabric.

034| How does an Indian living in the UK feel?

I have spent a few years living in London, and I can tell you that it's been one of the finest living experiences I can imagine. An Indian feels right at home. Connectivity to and from Britain is good across the globe, and that has positioned it as an important travel destination.

London was a stop-over hub for flights from Asia going to North America before long-haul flights came about. As a result, travellers would often make the most of their stop and enjoy what the country had to offer. This really attracted tourism. Today, however, there are longer and more direct routes.

Britain has seen glory during colonial rule, and that is still visible in London today, which in my view is the richest and the best European city. I would say it is my favourite city in the world, outside of my hometown of Mumbai.

Britain has some of the finest universities – Oxford, Cambridge, the London School of Economics and Political Science, the London Business School, Imperial College, Warwick University, University College London and many more.

Britain's economy is booming, making it one of the top ten economies in the world. Medical science in the country is advanced – it is a popular destination for medical tourism. From the best doctors to the best hospitals, Britain boasts of an excellent public health system – the National Health Service (NHS).

Summertime in London is brimming with life, with tourists from all over the world visiting. Hotel prices go up, and I have even seen Middle Eastern sheikhs bring their vehicles along with them. Britain has seen a lot of foreign investments in the last decade and a half. India's Tata Group has purchased Jaguar Land Rover and Corus Steel, and the Al Thani family of Qatar has invested in Harrods, the famous departmental store in Knightsbridge, London. Among the richest in the UK are Indians, and they have no issue with our culture or nationality. Locals, in fact, love Indians for the most part. So much so that in 2022, Rishi Sunak, a man of Indian origin, was elected prime minister of the country.

The Royal Family evokes pride in many British citizens, and one of the most beautiful areas of London is the one near Buckingham Palace. It is a pleasure to drive past it, and explore the parks and beautiful roads. When I was living in London, I had put up at central London, close to Green Park, and my Sundays would be spent just walking around in the area. I still cherish these fond memories.

Britain is full of history, and offers a lot of sightseeing options. In winter, skiing and other similar activities are also available. All in all, Great Britain is a superior functioning democracy, with people showcasing good manners and a good fashion sense. My overall experience of living there was great. A strong thumbs up to Britain – may their flag always fly high. I know there was a time when the sun never set on the British Empire, but today it has conquered all hearts, with its royalty and leadership wooing foreigners and locals with special warmth. Colonialism was a dark chapter in history and while it was a product of its time, I think it needs to be shunned from patriotic rhetoric for the sake of progress.

035| What does Australia have going for it?

Australia is part of the Commonwealth and the sixth largest country in the world by size. It boasts of an amazing culture centred on health and fitness, leading it produce the best sports teams and athletes in the world.

Australia has structured sporting bodies right from the school level to the inter-collegiate and professional levels. About twenty-four per cent of Australians over the age of fifteen participate in organized sporting activities. Rugby, soccer, cricket, swimming, tennis, surfing, horse racing, skiing and basketball are among the sports played there under an organized body. Australia has won the cricket World Cup five times, which is a world record in itself.

The lush greenery, the long summers and the encouragement for sports from a very young age, as well as ready sponsors, are responsible for Australians being good at various sports. The country has made huge investments in the domain of sporting infrastructure and that shows from its stadiums, which are some of the best in the world. Life expectancy in Australia in 2010 was 79.5 years for men, which is the third highest in the world, and eighty-four years for women, the seventh highest in the world. This can be attributed to their encouragement of physical activities, clean and green environment and low population, which allows quality medical care.

Australian citizens are often given health and education benefits and sometimes even monthly financial aid. The population of Australia is around 25 million, and the nominal GDP is roughly USD 1.725 trillion, with per capita GDP being around USD 65,000. This is as per data from 2022. Hence, it is a comparatively rich country. I feel like this country could take in some more immigrants and fully utilize the value of its vast lands. That would be my advice to the prime minister of Australia, if they were reading this. Given the weather conditions, it could be an amazing destination for industries and agriculture. There is further scope for Australia in the global economic race, and visiting the country is definitely on my bucket list.

036| Is Japan still the land of the rising sun?

Japan is an archipelago off the coast of East Asia, consisting of 6,852 islands. It has the eighth largest military in the world, which it maintains for peacekeeping and self-defence, often staying neutral in international affairs. The country has the third-largest nominal GDP of about USD 5 trillion and the twentieth-largest GDP per capita of around USD 35,000, as per 2022 data. Japan is the fourth largest exporter and importer of goods.

It is a constitutional monarchy and a sovereign state, but the power of the emperor is limited. The country enjoys excellent foreign relations with all the other countries, and the Japanese passport is among the most powerful in the world, wherein its citizens either get visa free entry or visa on arrival at over 190 countries. This is a huge feat, and it shows the excellence of its safety and crime index, which is the parameter countries would check before allowing any nation's passport holders to be given such access.

Japan is doing well economically and enjoys a healthy democracy. Sony, Lexus, Mitsubishi, Dai-Ichi Kangyo, Nomura, Softbank and Nippon are a few of the internationally acclaimed Japanese corporations. Earlier, Japan was a technological pioneer, being the only country with advanced technologies in many fields along with Germany, but now the playing field is more level, with more countries taking a leaf out of their book.

Nuclear power was a major source of power production, but the tsunami that hit Japan a few years ago resulted in leakage from one of its plants. As a result, the country has become more cautious. I believe this is just a temporary roadblock and the eco-friendly technology will once again boom.

Japan enjoys healthy tourism and is doing well in terms of agriculture and fishing. Buddhism is the predominant religion in the country. All in all, the land that gave the world bullet trains and popularized touchscreen technology, is staying ahead of the disruption curve, investing in research and development, all while staying high in the charts on global peace and stability. The Japanese have a very rich history and culture. Their culture also reflects in their management style in businesses.

Our group name, Enso, is a Japanese word that comes from the Zen sect of Buddhism. This is because of our admiration of the East and, in particular, the Japanese version of Buddhism.

037 | How is the Middle East gearing up for the green revolution?

The Middle East includes Bahrain, Egypt, Cyprus, Iran, Iraq, Israel, Jordan, Kuwait, Lebanon, Oman, Palestine, Qatar, Saudi Arabia, Syria, Turkey, the UAE and Yemen. Major wars have taken place in some of these countries and dictatorships have been uprooted to give people power through democracy.

Most of these countries are major oil and gas producers, leading to substantial development in the past. However, they have realized that hydrocarbons are a limited resource and that dependence on them is decreasing as cleaner and greener energy sources are being researched and used. To prepare for the future, the revenue from oil and gas is being reinvested into the development of infrastructure and tourist attractions. Additionally, local governments are attracting other industries so as to reduce the economic dependence on fossil fuels.

Most of these nations are Islamic theocratic states, and the people in this region are very pious. The issue is that these nations are a bit too conservative, with certain areas being notably patriarchal; in some of them sports and entertainment, especially for women, are not allowed and there are restrictions on free media reporting.

Some regions of the Middle East are amazing to visit, and the people are warm and friendly. For example, a favourite destination for shopping and entertainment is Dubai, a city in the UAE. Qatar recently has made visa-on-arrival possible for a bulk of countries, indicating an interest in promoting tourism. The 2022 Football World Cup took place in Qatar, and the nation spared no expense to create world-class infrastructure. Doha seems to be following suit when it comes to opening up for tourism and shopping.

A lot of hydrocarbon-rich economies have created state funds, such as the Dubai Investment Group (DIG) and Qatar Investment Authority (QIA), which invest in businesses globally. This is the best way to park and grow the capital they have gained from their rich oil and gas revenues over the years.

Overall, the Middle East of today is a peaceful region, barring Syria and Yemen, where there are issues with the ISIS militia. Iran is alleged to have been researching nuclear warfare technologies, however, the picture is not entirely clear regarding this. There is an embargo on Iran, and the country faces heavy sanctions from the USA. Yemen, too, went through recent turmoil over terror militia. The Palestine issue is long pending; let's hope a resolution is near. The Iraq war overthrew the cruel dictatorship of Saddam Hussein, and the country is known to be peaceful now.

Overall, the Middle Eastern countries are busy with their economic development, and collaborate on various issues from time to time, liberalizing their culture and overcoming religious dogma. I spent four months in Qatar as a student at Carnegie Mellon's Doha campus and absolutely loved the experience. I have also been a resident of Dubai for a brief period during my business career and liked the atmosphere and the piousness of Muslims there. It made me realize how

Islam is tarnished by fundamentalists and how serene most Muslims are.

I visited the Royal Palaces of Jordan due to business interests and found their richness, diversity and beauty extraordinary. I feel that Saudi Arabia, with its cash reserves, can achieve much more in terms of growth and development. Globalization is taking time to make a mark in the region, and while the UAE is way ahead of its time, others should follow suit and globalize. Doha would be the next most cosmopolitan city after Dubai.

A lot of universities and colleges have set up campuses in the Middle East upon invitation. The countries boast of strict laws and stricter law enforcement, and so they are largely crime free. The Gulf region is safe for women for the most part, but there are clothing and public display restrictions which are customary there. Drugs are a big no in all of the countries in the region and punishment for partaking in them is harsh.

038 | What can bring prosperity to the African continent?

There are fifty-four countries in Africa, and some of them struggle with poverty and large populations fighting to get even decent meals for survival, just like many rural places in India. Child mortality is also high in a few places, and diseases such as HIV, TB and cancer, which can be fatal, are rampant. The prevalence of polio and malaria has reduced, thanks to organizations such as the United Nations and the Bill & Melinda Gates Foundation that work relentlessly to eradicate these issues. Literacy and awareness are extremely low in the remotest regions of Africa. This part of the world needs care and uplifting. If a land is full of NGOs and other helping hands, it basically means that it is not at a stage where it should be and that there are problems that need fixing.

First of all, vigilance with regards to corruption has to be increased. This is one thing I have realized having worked in Guinea Conakry, where we had to face corrupt bureaucrats and saw corruption eating away at their resources like termites, at all levels. Large MNCs are digging for natural resources in these African countries, and although they are always bound by a Production Sharing Agreement (PSA), everything is known to be subject to change, such that everyone does what they like. The exploitation of Africa through cheap investments and expensive loans has been happening for years, and the country needs to put in place directives to prevent that. Nigeria is a large producer of oil and gas, but the situation there is dire too.

I feel the continent requires three things: quality investments to grow businesses, awareness of good farming methods and a strong anti-corruption drive. Philanthropists can take care of dire needs for some time, but who will oversee their work in the long run? It is better to teach people how to farm than hand them grains. Thus, it is best to intervene at the top level and enable the same process that has happened in neighbouring continents – the rise of strong and accountable governments. The people of the African democratic countries need to be made aware of their rights, and news media can be a powerful tool towards this endeavour.

South Africa, Egypt, Tanzania, Kenya and Mauritius are among the higher-grossing nations of Africa and receive tourists from around the world. These countries have done fairly well, but there is still a long way to go. The rate of crime is high in these countries too, and that is a big deterrent for tourists. Opportunities for jungle safaris and the general natural scenic beauty are in abundance, as are the vast pool of resources that can be harnessed to ramp up tourism.

Africa is an unsaturated market due to its low purchasing power parity (PPP). Thus, large companies still haven't gone in and set up shop. However, this would also put the region at risk of being exploited and treated as a large dumping ground. The preferred approach would be to get local businesses to flourish.

If a Samaritan were to ask me what we need to do to help Africa, I would say let's bring education, healthcare and good governance to these countries, along with investments for their businesses. Financial markets could be set up, and there is tremendous scope for cheap manufacturing, agro-products and natural resource conglomerates to grow there. Businesses will generate employment and, thus, an ecosystem for abundance.

Africa enjoys a long coastline, so freight transportation is possible. There are twenty-nine stock exchanges in Africa, representing the capital markets of thirty-eight nations

Accountability is low in Africa. Usually the citizens, including the average voter, are not satisfied with promises made that remain unmet. Consequently, there have been massive uprisings, which is a very good thing for democracy. The process of change is gradual, but to accelerate it, outsiders should intervene. Former British PM Tony Blair's 'Africa Governance Initiative (AGI)' is an excellent example of this.

039| What's scary about refugee migration?

As a result of the ongoing Arab spring and conflicts in the Middle East, hordes of refugees have migrated into Eastern and Southeastern Europe, with people fleeing from war-torn lands and seeking asylum. The crisis is so large and widespread that it is being compared to World War II. While the southeastern corridor remains open for refugees, countries are setting up camps at the borders to control them. A need for background checks has been felt, and the big question for them is whether these refugees will become an asset or a liability for their economy. These are important questions that must be pondered upon with empathy, and the pros and cons of absorbing the refugees should be weighed calmly.

What is more striking is that some countries like France and Germany have opened their arms to these people, many of them being women and children who have nothing left in their home countries and are not safe there. One thing that these European countries should bear in mind is that a lot of recent wars have had NATO participation, which means that the people are seeking refuge in the same countries that caused the destruction of their homelands and rendered them homeless. They are bound to hold grudges and hence, we see that ISIS is succeeding in influencing some individuals who end up waging lone wars on Europe, often killing many before they are shot dead themselves. Perhaps these are people who have lost the will to live. This is evident from the frequent one-off attacks in European countries, particularly in the UK, Turkey and France.

While I believe that we should open our arms and help these people since they have nowhere to go, they must be then be integrated into their new homes entirely, which changes the fabric of the host country. The USA has imposed strict guidelines for foreign immigrants due to threats of revenge violence. After all, their home countries were attacked.

The solution is to educate the refugees, heal them and give them a place where they can belong. That is why I say that a country should take in only as many people as it can handle and rehabilitate warmly and entirely. They will then integrate into the society and prove to be resourceful assets that could even become a part of the workforce.

The solution to the vast refugee migration crisis is to restore countries that have undergone destruction, and the right way to do that is to establish democracy, business, agriculture and growth in these lands. This can be achieved only through a unified effort by all. The issue should be taken up at the United Nations as well. With a coordinated effort, the next step towards making such places safe and bountiful should be taken, and these countries should be set on a path towards growth. Law and order should also be restored, and schools, colleges, hospitals and civic amenities must be set up, along with systems that can reintroduce peace and prosperity to their lands. People should be able to go back to their homelands and witness the progress that was ravaged because of the war. The peace process in the world is incomplete if a route to prosperity for these parts of the world is not carved out.

SOCIETY, CULTURE AND RELIGION

040 | What are the most habitually worrisome things for our future generations?

Think of the circumstances of our past generations and the high standards of excellence and sacrifice they have left us with. Would squandering it all away in revelry do justice to them? Would jeopardizing greatness for the subsequent generations to follow do them justice? Empires have collapsed when rulers have gone astray and indulged excessively. Rome fell due to inebriated rulers. We must be watchful of lowering standards and straying from the right path, a message that holds significance for all millennials.

Due to local trends and the liberal ideologies of the youth, parents find it difficult to stop their children from late nights out, partying, drinking, smoking or doing drugs. Divorce rates are soaring in different parts of the world, impacting even the more liberal societies. This is a global phenomenon. Cases of depression have gone up due to external pressures to conform, match others' standards and balance life's challenges and joys. Youngsters are often faced with conflicting routes and get lost midway.

The concerning thought is that life often revolves around superficial things, and there is little attention given to what truly matters. Today's youth is deeply entangled in the web of social media, competition and the race to get ahead.

It is good to be content and competitive. One has to balance the two. Bear in mind that an audience of hundreds and thousands of viewers on each post does empower young individuals, motivating them to perform their best online.

Living naturally, playing sports and not being glued to computer screens, OTT shows and movies would be a good way to lead a youthful life. Today, virtually everything is at our fingertips. However, we need to maintain our health, wealth and peace of mind by controlling our time on screens. After all, all work and no play make one a dull person.

041| Should gambling be legalized in India?

Gambling in India is heavily restricted except for selective categories, such as lotteries and horse racing. It is allowed offshore, which means that floating casino boats are legal. There are certain places in the country, such as Sikkim, from where you can run sports betting companies. Gambling in the US is restricted too, barring the Native American territories where it is legalized, such as Las Vegas in Nevada and Atlantic City in New Jersey. However, the law is lenient when it comes to online games involving money.

European countries, for the most part, allow gambling, and there are plenty of casinos. A casino usually has poker, blackjack, roulette and slot machines. Russia previously had restricted gambling zones but since 2009, it has made gambling legal nationwide. The Middle East restricts gambling as per the Islamic law.

Some of the African countries, especially the northern and western parts, are similar to the Middle East in terms of Islamic law governing them; in more liberal nations like South Africa, Mauritius, Nigeria and a few others, gambling is a huge tourist attraction. Singapore is a popular destination with plenty of casinos. Australia, too, allows casinos. China has a no-tolerance policy on gambling. In Hong Kong, social gambling is allowed, while casinos are restricted. Macau, an extension of Hong Kong and now a part of China, is full of flourishing casinos and is becoming a major gambling hub in Asia. Certain countries like Nepal have made gambling their unique selling point (USP), attracting people who come to gamble as their nearby home countries might not allow it.

Online gambling and betting are legal in many parts of the world where casinos aren't, but the legal framework still has to be set up properly. The minimum age for gambling almost everywhere is 18.

Although betting has been common since the dawn of civilization, people and governments have become aware of its pitfalls, and consequently, some have decided to curb it as much as possible. This was due to the fact that people, often inebriated, would lose a large part of their monthly incomes to these addictions.

I have gambled in many parts of the world, always within my limits, but have lost more than I have ever gained. As they say, in the end, the casino always wins. No matter how smart or savvy you are, it is a game governed by luck, and while some can afford to lose even millions in casinos, some can't afford to lose even 50 dollars. The job of the government is to look after the people at the bottom of the pyramid and hence, in my view, restricted gambling is better than an open door policy. The same applies to lotteries and betting on horse races.

My uncle and his friends, who fondly call themselves the 'Happy Club', often go on vacations to casino destinations. From personal experience, I can confirm that visiting the casino can be habit-forming. I remember sneaking out in the middle of the night in London and heading to the casinos at Leicester Square, even on work nights. Many times, I returned after losing some money to more experienced poker players.

Although gambling is illegal in India, during the festive season of Diwali, everyone plays *teen patti*, poker and blackjack. I feel that anything within limits is fine, but one mustn't cross the line or overdo it. Overall, till there is a safeguard against extreme poverty, legalization is a gamble in India.

042 | Are superstitions to be taken seriously?

By common logic, God, who controls destiny, obviously means well for all 'karmically good' people. Then why would there be superstitions to do with walking over a crack, walking under a ladder or Friday the 13th being an inauspicious date? I have realized that people are very superstitious, and folklore across the globe captures these superstitions. As a young kid, I too believed in deciphered signs from the unknown but, thankfully, I have changed and have resorted to a more logical approach to life.

In Mumbai, where I reside, there are some buildings in which the 13th floor is missing, and after the 12th comes the 14th floor. I find this so absurd that words can't describe how much I judge the builders who do this. People in India say that you should not get a haircut or cut your nails on Saturdays as it's inauspicious – as if cuttings nails or hair would summon a curse. Then there is the supposedly bad omen of a black cat crossing your path – my chauffeurs usually stop the car, reverse it and then move ahead – something I have asked them to not do. There are good omens too, such as a lizard falling on you or a bird dropping on you, which are supposed to bring luck. Just imagine!

People have to begin trusting their instincts and their ability to achieve goals and overcome their fears, rather than bickering about the things they hear. Form your own opinion, rather than trusting the unknown. There is another interesting ancient institution called *vastu*, which is similar to the Chinese *feng shui*, which serves as a guide for interior and exterior design and orientation of offices and homes. These experts decide which direction you should sleep in and how your furniture should be aligned.

People believe in numerology too, and that leads people to make modifications to their names or write it with suffixes and prefixes, a concept alien to me. There are gemstones and pearls that people wear to counteract the negative influence of planets in their horoscope, a practice I again find puzzling. Another belief is the significance of the number '1', which is often considered lucky. I have heard of people waiting for the clock to strike 11:11 or 1:11 before doing something important or getting their vehicle number plates to have '1' on them. In India, on auspicious days and birthdays, people would rather gift Rs 11,000 than Rs 10,000. Let me be clear that there is no superstitious reason for having 101 chapters in this book.

Signs and omens have been deciphered superstitiously since time immemorial, and people took major precautions in the past to follow these. Rulers had expert sages among their confidants and took their advice very seriously. The same has been true for many contemporary politicians and leaders, and that is appalling. Destiny, most definitely, is in one's hands and although, sometimes, these ancient arts may have some semblance of logic and truth in them, basing critical judgments or important decisions on them is a big no in my view. One should rely on everyday intelligence and common sense instead.

Religion to a large extent has civilized society and taught us to distinguish good from evil. I would say all gods were enlightened beings who preached similar teachings, albeit in different geographies, eras, languages and under different rules. A lot of gods who propagated religion are known to have been from the ruling class. People who get ahead in life definitely take moral guidance from faith but rely on their instincts and intelligence. Superstitions are not meant to be taken seriously.

043| Why learn about human psychology?

Social psychology was one of the best classes I took at CMU. It was followed by a psychology course I took at UC Berkeley, which I attended for summer school. The course was so interesting that I decided to follow it up with another one on the same topic at my home college. Some theories of social psychology are particularly interesting and when examined through a magnifying glass, can teach us a lot about how human beings operate in real life. Social psychology is defined as 'the scientific study of how people's thoughts, feelings, and behaviors are influenced by the actual, imagined, or implied presence of others. It studies conditions under which certain behaviours, actions, and feelings occur'. Let us look at some terms from the vast glossary of social psychology.

One of the most striking terms I came across was 'groupthink'. This is a tendency often observed when a group of people is deliberating over a topic for a while, such as in a long meeting, or are researching a topic for a length of time. Their ability to make decisions becomes obscured as they continuously revolve around the same ideas, and fatigue sets in. This tends to happen often, and in such cases, people need to call a time-out and find external support or fresh ideas. This applies to real-world workplaces in a big way.

Another interesting concept that struck me was the 'expectancy theory of motivation'. This theory states that people basically act in accordance with others' expectations of them and move forward with the intention of pleasing others with their outcomes. This tends to happen very often in the real world. A good example of this could be someone who habitually cracks jokes to get others to laugh at or with him. This theory is applicable to young people more than those who are older and have learnt to ignore the need for social validation.

Another striking theory of social psychology is the 'bystander effect', which explains how people are less likely to help someone in distress or in the case of an emergency if there are many people around. They tend to expect that someone else will take the leap. Since this is how most people think, the victim is abandoned in the same situation for a long time. It is important to see clearly and have an attitude of being the first mover.

Another striking theory is that of 'altruism', and this is one of my favourite phenomena. Andrew Carnegie, John D. Rockefeller, Bill Gates, Warren Buffet and Mark Zuckerberg from the US; Richard Branson from the UK; Azim Premji and Ratan Tata from India and many other multi-billionaires have gone down the path of philanthropy. This is altruism – doing something selflessly for others – and it has deep roots in society today. Our planet's future is brighter than ever before thanks to the philanthropy of the personalities named above and the hordes of other people who are inspired by them. They are putting their resources together and addressing the various problems of the world. Altruism means being charitable without expecting anything in return. One thing I know altruistic people get is an immense amount of admiration and good vibes from others. Well, if you induce smiles, then you receive smiles.

Another striking phenomenon that exists, even in some of the smartest people in the world, is the 'bias blind spot'. This term describes a situation when people become so self-righteous in their cognitive thinking that they believe that they cannot be biased, but fail to realize that their schemas (underlying thoughts) are founded on some biases that they are not aware of.

There is a whole glossary of terms in psychology and social psychology, and I have just shared just a few here. I would urge anyone still in college or school to take up this subject. Not only is this very interesting to study, it's also quite eye-opening. You could even study this topic online or purchase an entry-level book on it. This glossary and study will have real-life benefits and simplify one's thought processes, enabling better decision-making.

In a B2C business, people often market their products, which happens in B2B and B2G businesses as well, and knowledge of psychology is a pathway to understanding consumer behaviour and being good marketers.

044 | Why is it necessary to have a universal language?

The world is one today, and, according to me, this has been enabled, to some extent, by colonization. Most of the developed world has been bound by three common languages in which their laws are written: English, Spanish and French. There are many other languages, like Chinese, Japanese, Russian, Hindi, etc., but these are not internationally accepted. Modern research textbooks in almost all subjects are written, for the most part, in the English language, and we see that the language is being adopted by most of these countries with other linguistic traditions. I believe, it is high time that nations globally adopt English language education in the larger interest of the world's population. Internationalization is where most opportunities lie, and it will become possible only if people have access to all the modern data which is available in this language. English has evolved over a 1,400-year period and is the official language of sixty countries, with most others making it their second language.

While all other languages are valuable, if we are to solve the biggest challenges facing mankind, we have to meet somewhere in the middle on linguistics and knowledge communication media, and find a common language.

I think the one good that came of colonization, in hindsight, is the language they left behind in their colonies.

While I am fluent in English and Hindi, I can also speak some Marwari and understand Urdu. This makes my language skills versatile, but I strongly feel that English is the best bet for the overall unification of international society. The unification of the world is important, definitely more than our national or regional pride.

I hope it grows to become the universal language so that people from different parts of the world can converse and transact in it. People from a lot of countries don't speak English, which hinders them from browsing English journals and news media. I think this could change significantly in subsequent generations, and we are headed in the right direction. Research departments of many universities use English as their primary language, as does most of global media.

This essay would not be complete without mentioning that Mandarin is one of the most widely spoken languages, with approximately 1.2 billion fluent speakers. But that is owing to the large Chinese population, and the language is not as frequently spoken outside China. In India, there is immense diversity and although Hindi is prevalent, people speak other regional languages as well. There is beauty in diversity and people can only hope diversity is maintained within the bounds of ease of communication.

045 | How did racism begin and where is it headed?

One of my all-time favourite books is *A Place Called Freedom* by Ken Follett. The book reflects on the lives of slaves during colonial rule in the US and narrates how one slave escapes to freedom. Another good book is *Our Nig* by Harriet E. Wilson, which I read as a part of my coursework for an American History course at CMU. The history of slavery has been of great interest to me.

While Europe was booming with riches and glory, African nations suffered from poverty and were victims of disdain. During colonial conquests, there was a need to row ships, clean surfaces, wash clothes and do menial tasks that required manual labour and physical strength. Mining required strong hands and plantations, workers. Thus, white people often engaged in slave trade. The slaves were shipped off to colonies, where typically the British, French, Spanish, and Portuguese ruled and proudly hoisted their flags. Many African countries were colonies too. The slaves had no way of breaking free; anyone who tried to flee was either shot dead or arrested. They had no basic human rights and were treated as the physical property of either their colonial rulers or plantation owners.

But Africans were not the only race who were so treated. Indians too were bought as slaves by the Mughal and British rulers and deported to various parts of the world. That is also why there are so many people of Indian and African descent in different parts of the world, with large Indian communities found in Indonesia, Malaysia and Mauritius.

This oppression reached a pinnacle some centuries ago and was followed by an age of revolts. The slaves were miserable and wanted equal rights. Many influential people joined their cause to end racial discrimination. This primarily happened towards the end of the nineteenth century. Later, South Africa witnessed the Apartheid, where Black and white people had different rights. Mahatma Gandhi was kicked out of a train for being brown, and this affected him greatly. He realized the power of unified movements through his intelligent non-violent campaign against Apartheid in this African country first and the freedom movement in India much later.

Nelson Mandela fought for the rights of black people in South Africa, which led to his imprisonment. He was later released and went on to lead the country. People like Martin Luther King Jr. and Rosa Parks led the movement in the US. Together, oppressed people fought in different ways and in different parts of the world to send out the message that the time had come for the end of slavery. In December 1865, the ratification of the Thirteenth Amendment of the American constitution formally ended the legal institution of slavery throughout the country. Abraham Lincoln, the thirteenth US President, was ahead of his time and wanted the concept to disappear. The world followed his example to abolish slavery and slowly integrate these people into mainstream society.

Today, we can tentatively say that we have come a long way, and deep oppression has brought forth many thinkers and achievers. Barack Obama became the forty-fourth US

President, holding one of the most powerful public offices in the world. His origins are in Kenya in Africa and his election marked a great moment in history.

They have faced unparalleled oppression through centuries. There is a lot of hope for a day when racism, still a persistent issue, will be history. There is still discrimination against people of many races in different parts of the world, and demographically they form the weaker section of society. Africa is still in turmoil, and as a result, many African countries to suffer from poverty. Gradually, with good governance, healthcare, nutrition and education, they will come out strong. They have a lot to offer to the world, and it all begins with equal rights.

046| Are men and women really equal today?

The global population is estimated to have an almost equal ratio of men to women (102 men to 100 women). In such a setting, if approximately fifty per cent of the population of the world is not given equal opportunity, it is a huge loss to the human race. Today's women are educated and well-read, and equal pay is their fundamental right. Women often face pay discrimination and that is unfair as their contribution, from general observation, is as good as men's, if not better.

Anthropologically, women have always been forced to stay behind. When men were hunters and gatherers or farmers, women were nurturers of children. They often don't, have the same physical strength as men, but many jobs today don't require physical labour, so this is no longer a drawback. In the realm of dating, chivalry originated with the logic that men were the providers and women the pleasers. However, today's women like to pay their share of the cheque and expect equal treatment.

I have always been against putting my children in an all-boys or all-girls school or college. I don't think that their upbringing is complete without interactions between the two genders and believe in the co-ed system for their development. Boys and girls need to learn to be around each other and be comfortable with the opposite gender.

Our society cannot function effectively when women aren't given equal opportunities. We live in a world of strong role models like Angela Merkel, Theresa May, Indira Gandhi, Mother Teresa and Rosa Parks, and more alpha-females who have created lasting change. Their stories should inspire today's women. The current call for gender equality, I think, will be answered and become a reality soon.

Some parts of the world, such as Saudi Arabia, are extremely patriarchal even today, where women have only now been allowed to drive cars. Malala Yousafzai and Narges Mohammadi, awardees of the Nobel Peace Prize, along with Claudia Goldin who was awarded the Nobel Prize for Economics for her paper on gender disparity in labour markets, are beacons of hope for innumerable people leading research and good work. Malala fought hard for equal education rights in Pakistan even in the face of a life threat from the Taliban. Narges is an Iranian human rights activist. There are many more champions of this cause even where religious bigotry does not allow women to come into the limelight. Men and women also need to respect boundaries while interacting, as it is not the same as interacting with their own gender. Often, disrespect causes discomfort, but that is fast changing as more and more women are joining the workforce around the world.

047 | Should abortion and prenatal gender determination be legal?

India banned pre-natal gender determination in 1994 through the Pre-Conception and Pre-Natal Diagnostic Techniques Act. I don't think we can get more regressive than that. Such a restriction is unheard of in other parts of the world, and expecting parents who want to know the gender of the foetus can travel overseas and do it anyway. Sometimes, doctors oblige out of a sense of camaraderie or for money, and corruption abounds in sonography or ultrasound clinics.

Italy is home to the Vatican City, a separate country within the geographic boundaries of Rome. The country is largely under the influence after Catholicism and allows abortion only in the first ninety days after conception. This is the case for most of Europe. The USA was completely liberal for a long time and allowed an abortion at any stage, no matter how late, but the country went back on this ruling recently across some states, sparking an important debate.

Restrictive policies are regressive. Who is the State to tell citizens what they should do when it comes to family planning? I think abortion and gender determination are fundamental rights of a human being, and no one should have the directive to supersede them. Sometimes, abortion is necessary to safeguard the health of the mother, sometimes a change in the financial circumstances of the family may require it. The State should not infringe upon people's decision-making.

048 | Are prostitution and pornography healthy for society?

Objectifying men and women has been a terrible idea right from the start. Our generation has a higher divorce rate than the previous ones, with more dissatisfied men and women who seem to have lost the understanding of the sanctity of marriage. What is the reason for this? Our generation has been exposed to pornography, nudity and has had easy access to sex. None of these are looked down upon or frowned upon. *Au contraire*, people are mocked for not having seen pornography or entered a strip club in their lives. At one point, these activities were considered sanctimoniously wrong.

Sex tourism has become a new culture. Many countries like Netherlands, Thailand, Belgium, Russia, the UK, Switzerland, Singapore and Australia have made prostitution legal. Pornography is legal in almost all countries, leading youngsters to be exposed to explicit content and its sexual realities from a very young age. As a result, they explore their sensuality when they are young. Masturbation, however, is known to be healthy, and most adolescents engage in it. This results in an early desire to form sensual bonds, and that leads to multiple sex partners. This is acceptable as long as it doesn't result in a dissatisfaction with a single partner after marriage. Breaking marital ties is problematic and especially for children, who witness strained relationships, and in some instances, their parents' separation or divorce.

Prostitution is rampant, and working men often cheat on their wives. This culture has broken the fabric of society and needs to be mended. I might sound conservative, but strip clubs and pornography can have a negative effect on people's minds, leading them to see the opposite gender as mere objects of gratification as opposed to meaningful companions. Past generations were able pass down some values because they often had a secure and sound married life.

I am glad to be living in India, which has a conservative approach to these things. With the advent of the internet, pornography has gained a vast market online where earlier video cassettes called 'blue films' dominated the market, followed by DVDs. Pirated downloads started further increased variety and accessibility, and turning it into a flourishing industry with popular sites adding videos every minute.

Illegal prostitution can be bad for multiple reasons. In countries where sex tourism is allowed, there is regular and periodic AIDS and HIV testing. If you are caught with a prostitute, the only consequence is shame. But in case you are caught with a prostitute in a country where it isn't legal, you could be jailed. Sexually transmitted diseases (STDs) are a risk everywhere, as the infection can be caught even if you are exposed to it only once.

Let's hope we can provide a better and morally sound future for upcoming generations by deliberating on the new and rapidly evolving culture, which I feel is excessively liberal. Evolve for the better.

049 | How bad are drinking and smoking as habits?

Andrew Carnegie once said that a person with self-respect wouldn't enter a pub or a bar. I think his point was that such places are associated with a 'dark' way of life. We associate drinking and smoking with ill-health for sure, but also with ill minds. Consuming some alcohol for recreation could be relaxing, but falling into a vicious cycle of clubbing and partying at any age is not conducive to a healthy future. It can become a breeding ground for a self-indulgent and unproductive frame of mind, whereas people who are focused on their careers are improving their lives through creating, developing, hustling and nurturing.

It is well known that drinking can be a depressant, as it affects the brain cells. It can also be habit-forming and definitely changes your sleep cycle, which is bad for productivity. Countries have determined different minimum ages to buy liquor. In the UK, it is sixteen (for beer, wine or cider) or eighteen, in the USA, it is twenty-one and in India, it is twenty-five. This shows that careful thought has been put into discourage youngsters from picking up glasses in some countries, while others have been historically more liberal.

People can black out by consuming too much alcohol and unknowingly commit heinous crimes, for which they may have to pay all their lives. They could get into fights, or if they get behind the wheel, they could be hazardous for their and others' lives. If you are drinking, drink responsibly. Know your limits and do not get drunk.

Smoking often follows drinking at a young age. It is very addictive and terrible for your lungs, reducing your stamina. No one ever notices, but it is a terrible distraction and a complete waste of time. Smokers at workplaces or in colleges have to step out of their buildings to smoke and then walk back in. That can take up to tent to fifteen minutes. The process is then repeated multiple times a day. It is terrible for people who work out, and for libido and sperm cells.

Lung cancer is one of the most fatal forms of cancer, especially if detected late. So beware smokers; if you develop cancer anywhere between your throat and lungs, you might leave your near and dear ones mourning your loss for the rest of their lives. Smoking is bad for people around you as well. Earlier, people could smoke in public places, but thankfully that is not the case anymore. The norm is that there is no more passive smoking unless you are in a designated smoking section now.

While drinking is relatively easier to give up, smoking requires a lot of effort. There are plenty of self-help books available to help someone who wants to quit. You could resort to electronic cigarettes for a while, but they are harmful too. Alternatively, use nicotine gum or nicotine patches to substitute the physical requirement for nicotine. Quit immediately if you are addicted, as smoking could get you into a lot of trouble. Mahatma Gandhi had an even more drastic response to smoking, saying that it could lead a person to commit crimes. Well, I'm not sure about that, but smoking is indeed a terrible habit. Quit today.

050 | Should cannabis be made legal everywhere?

Some countries have legalized the use of marijuana. Tremendous research has been conducted in this field, and there are mixed opinions regarding the exploitation of this plant. The issue is further complicated as it is a controversial topic. Some states in the USA have legalized its recreational use too. Medicinal marijuana is used to treat lung disorders like bronchitis.

I personally believe that any form of the substance is bad and am against its usage. It is a gateway drug to other, more potent, drugs and can prove to be lethal and habit-forming. I know of people who began taking marijuana in school and college and moved on to experiment with cocaine, MDMA, acid, heroin and so on. Before they knew it, they ended up in rehab or with mental illnesses resulting from addiction. When you start indulging in these activities, you may form groups or cliques. Cannabis is known to lower productivity and could even distract you from your professional and educational goals. Just like alcohol, almost all drugs are addictive.

I can tell you with some confidence that almost all colleges around the world have a lot of drug users. All the time spent in these activities could have been used instead for developing skill sets. Tobacco is often consumed along with cannabis. There is a notion that marijuana makes you more creative, and people romanticize this idea but it is a false one – not everyone can become Leonardo Da Vinci by consuming drugs. Marijuana is known to damage brain cells.

Legalization of lower-class drugs, if at all, should be done with extreme caution and a lot of education. They should never be institutionalized and, more importantly, just like cigarettes, there should be campaigning against its usage.

Some countries have legalized marijuana for recreational use to attract tourists, without realizing that the future generations in their country will suffer greatly with their so-called 'liberal approach' to cannabis usage. It could be detrimental to society. The excuse often cited is that the underworld market for these drugs can be done away with it if they are given a legal place, but I think that is worse, as there will be no check on its consumption at all. Think of the number of cases in newspapers of overdose and deaths. Cannabis may not directly lead to death by overdosing, but increased intake of many other drugs could prove fatal. Drugs should be regulated, even if legalized.

051 | How can we help transgender people?

Transgender people are in the minority and are born with a biological aberration. There is nothing they can do to change themselves, and gender affirmative or hormonal treatments are not always entirely successful. Given this reality, society must create awareness and make a place for them.

Transgender people do not have the same access as cisgender people to schools, colleges, jobs or a regular social life because they face discrimination. Many such individuals get engaged in commercial sex work (CSW) to make a living and live a very challenging, detached life from society.

In today's day and age, where more and more marginalized communities are finally getting equal rights and status, we must ensure that trans people get theirs too. I strongly think that the Indian transgender population should be given a quota in education and careers. The hijra community in India is often found asking people for money either on the streets or family functions and this is how most of them make ends meet. Just imagine what that must do to their sense of self-respect. The situation could be better in other parts of the world, but I believe it most certainly is not as good as it should or could be.

Governments should help initiatives and NGOs working to further the transgender community's cause, so they can build a future for themselves. It is appalling to see people mock them. In today's generation, as awareness grows, we see empathy and consensus for them growing. However, our goal should not only be that of empathy towards them, rather of equal opportunities, rights and a respectable life just like the one we have for ourselves. They are people too and deserve every joy meant for cisgender men and women. We will see accelerated change; I am confident of that.

During Donald Trump's term, the transgender population was banned from joining the armed services. Joe Biden reversed the ban. I believe that humanity sometimes comes at a cost, which we should not hesitate to bear.

052 | How can we make homosexual people feel more accepted in society?

Homosexuality is legal in most parts of the world. However, same-sex marriage is not yet legal in as many countries. There is no doubt in my mind that a person's right to love someone, irrespective of their gender, is a personal choice, and we must have a liberal outlook. Queer people are in the minority, and there's a strong lobby base to accept them and give them the same place in society as 'straight' men and women.

In some countries, it is still a crime to be gay, lesbian or bisexual. Where it's legal, it's looked down upon by a vast majority of people. Liberal individuals realize that that it is their personal preference or choice, and everyone must be accepting of that. India decriminalized of gay sex recently, and I couldn't be prouder.

At workplaces, people often discriminate and close the doors to opportunity for people based on their sexual orientation, and I think that stems from a lack of thoughtfulness. Feeling shame and being unable to accept one's sexuality is becoming less common, thanks to the bold men and women who have come out of the closet. Tim Cook, the Apple CEO, is openly gay; Karan Johar, a successful Indian film director and producer, is openly gay and people love him. These are two of my favourite examples, but similarly, there are many gay, lesbian and bisexual people who now have a safe passage to a sound life.

My advice to you is that if you feel your sexuality is stifled in your country or place of origin because the government is under the influence of religion or the laws don't support your orientation, then, if possible, you must migrate to another country where you can be yourself. People can sink into depression by suppressing their sexuality.

One of my best friends from my childhood was gay, Today, I am glad he can proudly wear the badge of his sexual orientation. Live and let live. Love is love. Let your pride flag fly high.

053 | Why is there a red tape on sex education?

It is imperative for children to learn the secrets of childbirth, but this topic is often not addressed by parents or teachers in our country. In many parts of the world, sex education is a part of the school curriculum, enabling the youth to engage in intercourse in a planned and educated way. Till about the ninth grade, I was clueless about sex, and I remember an instance when my friends laughed at me. All children should be taught enough to avoid embarrassment and misinformation.

There are many parts of the world that are conservative in their educational approach due to theocratic influences or because they lean to the political right. But it's important to educate children about reproduction, effective usage of condoms and birth control pills and the prevention of sexually transmitted diseases (STDs). The age of consent in most countries is sixteen or eighteen. Some theocratic countries like Saudi Arabia do not allow sex before marriage. While these rules are often broken, I think it is important to allow people to make an informed decision.

In-depth sex education most definitely needs to be a part of the school curriculum. This is a must to avert unwanted pregnancies and the transmission of STDs. Teaching the children how to use contraceptives, among other things about sex, is their parents' job too.

054 | How has globalization shaped and transformed cultural boundaries?

I attended a lecture in college where the professor, an author, stated that culture evolves towards economically superior societies. I find that partially true, but not entirely. Cultural transfusion has been taking place for a long time, as people interact and influence each other, and this has accelerated as the world has shrunk to fit into a smartphone. Think about how many civilizations have existed over the centuries, and now how many countries exist. You will find that the number of countries is smaller than the number of civilizations.

In hindsight, this amalgamation has happened with the passage of time, as weaker communities got annexed by the stronger ones. Christians, Muslims and Buddhists sent missionaries to conquered lands, and that was the tipping point of cultural change. Soon the change spread to clothing, eating habits, languages, art, music, drama – you name it.

These inventions date back to the 19th century, and so we will consider that as the beginning of major cultural changes. The real cultural differences between nations began reducing with the advent of television, radio, newspapers, magazines and the internet.

Long before these great inventions, there was the colonial era. Wherever colonial powers, mostly European, established their rule, the local cultures were subjected to theirs as well.

However, initially, the colonized resisted the changes. In most colonies the vast majority of people stood their ground, wanting these rulers out. There were persistent movements, both violent and non-violent, where they fiercely fought against the exploitation by these foreign forces. I have always maintained that this topic should be examined through the lens of history. There were pros and cons to this era of human history. Portugal, Spain, France and Britain – the main European superpowers of the time – were really advanced industrialized economies. They greatly sped up the development in their colonies too. However, they were outsiders, and the colonized wanted their freedom. Hence, they united against them. In India alone, all the states ruled by local rulers joined forces against a common outsider, whom they viewed as their shared enemy. I find this important to mention because some of the regions were Muslim-dominated while others were Hindu-dominated representing the two most widespread religions of India. South America and North America were primarily Christian, while Africa was primarily Muslim.

With colonial rule came three dominating languages – Spanish, French and English – taking the place of the many native tongues. That was the first cultural change. European dining and clothing habits also spread to these colonized countries, with the local populations adopting them at a rapid pace. This transformation unfolded over a period of years, spanning centuries.

The USA, which gained freedom on 4 July 1776, was a large landmass with a small local population of indigenous people when Europeans arrived nearly three centuries ago. When the colonies gained independence, the newly liberated population also comprised of Europeans who had settled there and sought freedom from the rule of the land of their forefathers. The remaining population, consisting of Black people, were originally slaves brought from Africa to perform physical labour under colonial rule. Although they were eventually freed, it took a long time for them to gain equal rights. They had a different culture that was amalgamated with the local White culture.

While America doesn't have a history spanning millennia as Europe does, it has a culture similar to that of Europe. Americans, in my opinion, were not as influenced by the church as Europeans, and hence are more liberal, which I think has been the reason for their success. The land is called the 'free world' and has done extremely well economically for decades. Today, the biggest cultural influencers are the Americans, with their film industry, Hollywood, and their music reaching all over the world. American English differs from British English, and Americans have maintained the differences between Celsius and Fahrenheit, miles and kilometres, as well as left-hand and right-hand driving.

With the rise of various kinds of media, including inventions such as television, radio, newspapers, magazines and the internet, global ideologies have split between East and West. While the East has been known to be hierarchical, with close-knit families, patriarchal and 'conservative' in their approach to life, the West has been seen as more 'liberal' – easy-going, characterized by universal suffrage, less pious and non-patriarchal. Today, Western culture has risen to a dominating position in society, and Eastern cultures are viewed as exotic. Has superior economic power succeeded in transforming or converting the older cultures?

People have automatically and freely adopted Western culture. This doesn't imply that they are mindless, but rather that the influence of Western culture has rubbed off on the rest of the world in a big way, leading to people from various cultures to desire the things that it offers.

Asian local attire has almost become history, and people dress in suits, speak English, listen to Western music and watch Hollywood films. The East has also become less hierarchical and more easy-going. That is one thing I am happy about.

There is immense beauty in diversity. Today, due to this diversity, multiple cuisines are found in all cities around the world – Japanese, Chinese, Thai, Italian, Indian, Burmese, Continental, French and so on. I suppose, in this culinary richness, everybody wins.

Cultural attributes, like religious beliefs, are a personal choice, and we must be respectful of that. The sole purpose of this chapter is to reflect on how cultures have influenced each other and how the world is overcoming cultural boundaries. In the modern era of social media, we have to understand that everything is up for a fair trial, and people have a right to choose and pick. Culture should not be imposed through unwanted laws, even though religion and culture often have a way of influencing the rule book.

055 | What are the advantages of a monogamous life?

The secret to a fruitful life is a happy marriage, healthy children and a career that brings you joy and provides the means to sustain your lifestyle. People have often mentioned that the secret to success lies in happy familial bonds, as they offer a tremendous amount of support. However, I personally find the current state of affairs quite chaotic and often wish we could turn back time. Honestly, I would feel much safer about raising my kids in a previous generation, albeit with the benefits of present technological advances.

In India, my home country, there are two kinds of marriages – love and arranged. Love marriages have become as common as arranged marriages now, following a pattern similar to any other country: two people meet, fall in love and build a life together. In the case of arranged marriages, meetings are set up with a series of potential partners, and families arrange a marriage with whoever the person clicks with. In the case of arranged marriages, parents or professional matchmakers play Cupid. To those unfamiliar with the concept it may seem awful, but arranged marriages are not inherently negative. I have been asked about this concept a ton of times by my foreign friends, as they find it intriguing. It certainly is commercialized, as brokers charge an initial fee to take up a case or a success-based fee or both, however, their role is confined to setting up the initial meeting. Ultimately, the boy and the girl decide with their families. *Indian Matchmaking*, a popular OTT show, is quite an accurate depiction of what arranged marriages look like.

In the days of my grandparents and earlier, youngsters were not given many options and tied the knot at a very young age, sometimes while still in school. Families fixed the marriages, and the couple met each other only during the wedding. Child marriage is now abolished, and I often share jokes about this aspect with my grandparents.

It takes compatibility to make a marriage work and thus, I believe couples should invest enough time in understanding each other before they decide to get married. That is a must. Following that, they should remain loyal to each other and work together as a team, looking after each other. They should plan their family together, respecting each other's perspectives, and try to accommodate each other's preferences as far as possible, making compromises when necessary. That is what a relationship is all about. Your spouse should be your best friend.

Personally, I would prefer my partner to be a career-oriented person. That way, we will have a lot to talk about and share at the end of the day.

While I might sound like I have everything planned, I am very concerned about the generational shift towards trial and error and hope that experimentation doesn't lead future generations astray. Values are, thus, very important to instill, and leading by example is the most effective way to do so. We shouldn't expose children to foul language and bad habits, making them believe that it's acceptable to do things that are considered *passé* today. There will come a time when we have to educate them about everything relevant to their lives, things we might have hidden from them until then, and that's when you become their friends. Taking time out for your children, holidaying with them, and getting involved with them are crucial steps to make them feel comfortable to share their thoughts and feelings with you, be honest with you and know that you will support and guide them.

Nowadays, a lot of marriages end up in divorce, and that is a sad state of affairs. I blame that on liberalization and the widespread acceptance of almost everything, whether it's wrong or right. Just imagine the distress caused to young children whose parents separate. I am happy to have been brought up by two amazing parents who showed us the power of love and commitment through the strength of their bonds. I would want to do the same for my children.

Always be certain before you commit to marriage, and once you are in, you have to give each other space and understand that your single life won't return, no matter how much you might miss it. But your partner can be your best friend, someone you can confide in, discuss and celebrate the little joys with all your life. That person should be your backbone. Do not betray your partner under any circumstances and keep the trust and love alive.

If your family life is set, you will have the time and mental space to work on bigger and better things, and maybe put a dent in the universe.

056| Is fanfare around celebrities justified?

Since childhood, I have been lucky enough to have met accomplished people, champions in their respective fields – celebrities, businessmen, sportsmen, politicians, artists, etc. I think that commendable achievements, across different fields, are amazing and should be lauded. However, the continuous hounding of these alpha achievers is tragic, especially in a country like India.

Where poverty and illiteracy levels are high, people tend to develop greater excitement levels around public figures. This applies mainly to lower income countries, as opposed to high-income countries. In Mumbai, where the who's who of India live, we see that crowds surround celebrities, often acting uncouth and desperate to catch a glimpse of them, pestering them for a photograph for their social media pages or an autograph. Sometimes they just want to shake hands. The celebrities are also rude or dismissive sometimes, but I don't think they are completely at fault here, as it must be exhausting to be welcoming of strangers all the time.

In developed countries, on the other hand, where people have higher income and education levels, celebrities can walk around more freely as it is generally considered rude to disturb them. People contain their excitement instead of mobbing them, and manners are upheld. That is what should be followed everywhere. People should be self-respecting.

Maybe some celebrities like the fanfare to some extent, but to a layman like me it seems like an unnecessary craze.

Following celebrities on social media is a decent way to show your appreciation for their work, but trolling their personal remarks and being abusive, online or offline, is a big no-no. These people have a right to their opinion and will exercise it as they like. Who are we to dissuade them from doing so?

Some celebrities attract huge crowds and are treated like demigods. So much so that the paparazzi and even the educated folks don't spare them. There is a 'media factory' that feeds on celebrity gossip too. That is just unhealthy, and people shouldn't be put on a pedestal, so much so that their personal lives become a spectacle for the laymen and their daily conduct is filmed for daily consumption on TV. There is enough current news and a wide range of problems that can be reported. That is what good journalism ought to be focusing on.

Celebrity marriages are a feast for the paparazzi, where the celebs too exploit this behaviour to sell coverage rights to magazines and the media, sometimes charging millions. We need to have a new normal, where appreciation doesn't turn into an annoyance for people.

057 | Are all religions similar?

I was born and raised in a Hindu Jain family. Hindus are generally polytheistic, and Jains believe in 'karma'. I always followed Hindu Jain values and beliefs and remained strictly vegetarian, but something has changed. I have begun questioning my beliefs about the remainder of the value system of all religions in general.

The majority of the world follows the Christian faith. Other religions include Islam, Judaism, Buddhism and more. How can it be that one faith is right and others wrong? How can there be just an Allah or Ram but no Christ, or to put it mildly, who is right between Prophet Mohammed, Christ, Ram or Mahavira?

I now believe – and I sound like a character in a Dan Brown novel – that there definitely is a strong karmic law that governs the universe. All these gods and deities seemed to be spiritually elevated or enlightened beings, but they communicated with the same universal power that others did. Their original teachings probably got lost or diluted in the sands of time. They may have simply deciphered their spiritual beliefs differently given the eras they existed in, which did not have modern modes of efficient communication. Their geographies and chronologies were different too. No one religion is a hundred per cent accurate, according to me.

I don't believe in life after death or heaven and hell, but

I do believe in karma. The concept is simple – do good, and good shall be done to you. There is enough evidence to show that there are structures at locations where these 'gods' lived and a lot of religious fervour around certain parts of the world. Research has shown that there is evidence to support the idea that prophets and spiritual leaders existed. However, could it be that they saw the same enlightened vision as each other, just to different degrees? That would mean there is only one truth.

Historically and anthropologically, I strongly believe that religion has been the biggest cause of war and conflict, but it has also led human beings to think about right and wrong, giving them a moral compass and a sense of direction. The rest is history or mythology. There seems to be power in some mantras or chants, owing to certain metaphysical phenomena that result from them, and the energy they generate travels. I believe in a grand design – in the larger scheme of things of this universal power that guides us upwards and wants to engulf us with its limitless and infinite power. The universe would want that, after all.

058| What is a vegetarian's monologue?

I am vegetarian, but I know that those who eat meat love it. On the other hand, I also know people who have turned vegan and still manage to have an uncomplicated diet. Homo sapiens have been eating meat since the days of hunters and gatherers. Agriculture began much later. However, because of certain religious institutions, many turned vegetarian as killing animals, birds or fish was viewed as a sin.

The majority of the world eats non-vegetarian food products, but people are increasingly becoming aware of the negative effects of eating too much meat. Animals, poultry and fish often carry diseases that can be transmitted to the people consuming them. My reasoning to stay vegetarian is partly my upbringing and partly the fact that I realize how much pain is caused to the animals when they are killed for consumption. The simple sight of it sometimes makes me wonder, what if that were to happen to me? What if I was lower down in the food chain?

A vegan diet is extremely tough to maintain, but there is a similar feeling of compassion for other living creatures behind it. Cows, buffaloes and goats are kept away from their mothers after birth so the milk can be extracted for human consumption. I find that preposterous, for a mother can only feel pain at being kept away from their progeny. The animals are often injected with steroids for a higher dairy output and are made to undergo multiple pregnancies, which is cruel. When I heard about this for the first time from a dear friend, I decided to reduce my dairy consumption.

People for the Ethical Treatment of Animals (PETA) is the largest animal rights organization in the world, with more than 6.5 million members and supporters. They are actively working and have succeeded in communicating their point to a large extent. Increased awareness about animal cruelty is making people turn vegetarian and vegan, and for that I am happy.

There is another section of the population that call themselves pescatarians, and these are people who eat fish, but no meat. Well, I think fish feel pain too when they are taken out of the water, and their death is like that of any other species. Right?

059 | How beautiful is Islam in reality?

According to me, Islam is a very pious religion. I haven't seen followers of any other religion follow their faith so diligently. Whenever I have visited Amman, Doha, Dubai or any other place in the Middle East, I have been awestruck by people calmly following their faith. Speaking to the locals, I realized that they are very worried about the state of their faith today and how it looks outside the confines of their land.

Ramadan is a month when Muslims fast, and being Jain, I see the same fervour among people of my faith. But we are not as many in number as the Muslims, and the same intensity is not maintained all year around, as in the case of Islam, where most believers do *namaz* five times a day.

Peaceful Arab nations perceive terrorism as a threat to their religion and its reputation. Personally, I have studied a bit of the Quran and the Bible, as both the holy books have found a place on our shelves. I have realized that there is one thing common in these two books and almost all religious doctrines – the definitions of good and bad. Some religions preach birth and rebirth, while some talk about heaven and hell, but the good conduct is always defined by good deeds, honesty and piety.

During my student days at Carnegie Mellon's Doha campus, I used to see how local students would pray at their designated times as the azan would be blasted on the speakers in the college building. Islamophobia exists because of the misdeeds of a few people who have chosen intolerance as a path. They are usually from the poorer sections of society and are lured to take on guns in the name of the holy religion.

Al Qaeda and ISIS have no clear objective, in my mind. They just want to prove their mettle and, lacking a better claim to fame, have taken up weapons under the disguise of 'jihad'. Real Islam preaches tolerance, and I have Muslim friends who are really good, kind people. In India, which is a secular state, I witness each day how much humanity exists in Muslims due to their pious habits.

I don't agree with slitting the throats of goats or polygamy, but that is just my view as a vegetarian monogamist. Thumbs up to Islam, for it is a peaceful, loving and nurturing faith that has given direction to its millions of followers and continues to be a beacon of hope for people struggling in their daily lives. Faith makes people delve within, which is why we must give respect to every religion and give its followers their due place. Religion usually is a very personal aspect of life.

The actions of a select few must not lead us to misconstrue the entirety of a religion. While Islamophobia exists, I am sure it will vanish in the near future, when these 'rascals' who are ill-portraying an entire community are eradicated.

060 | How is the Christian demographic faring?

Christianity is a monotheistic religion, based on the teachings of Jesus Christ. It is the most widely followed religion in the world, with over thirty-three per cent of the global population identifying as Christians. The Bible is the holy book of Christianity and is considered sacred. The religion is followed in over two-thirds of all countries in the world, covering a population of 2.4 billion people.

Four of the largest branches of Christianity are:

1. The Catholic Church with 1.3 billion people
2. Protestantism with 920 million people
3. The Eastern Orthodox Church with 260 million people
4. Oriental Orthodoxy with 86 million people.

The Pope in the Vatican City is the head of the Catholic Church. Christianity is considered one of the most peaceful religions. Most of the West follows this faith. Since the West comprises the most developed parts of the world, we see frequent mentions of Christianity in books and movies that originate there.

The religion has been a light for billions of people across the globe since time immemorial. Historically, peaceful missionaries have been sent out to foreign lands by rulers to convert people to this faith. Holy wars or crusades too have occurred in the name of Christianity, but those happened long back in history.

Churches exist in all parts of the world and showcase some of the best styles of architecture. Christmas, celebrated on 25 December, is the day Jesus Christ was born. Christmas may just be the most widely celebrated holiday in the world, with people of all religions revelling with the Christians. This is largely due to the soft power of the religion, in that it doesn't believe in controversial intrusions or forceful practices, while working in the larger interest of all.

Back in the day, missionaries often forcefully converted people, but that has long ended and people have evolved. European nations often established churches in their colonies, spreading the religion far and wide.

In my view, Christians have understood the true meaning of practising a religion, and that shows amply in the geopolitical arena. I attended a Catholic school for two years and read William Shakespeare's *Merchant of Venice*, an amazing insight into the Christian world. Wherever you go in Europe, you will see the stamp of Christianity. Christians are one of the kindest people I can think of, people who care deeply about others. They are not as bigoted as people of some other religions either. Maybe there are some outliers to this perception, but this is a common observation. Owing to the prosperity in Christian-dominated societies, they are also sometimes the most altruistic. In the list of billionaires who have signed up for the Giving Pledge, most people are of this faith.

061 | What is the state of Hinduism in India?

Hinduism is a polytheistic religion, which means that the Hindu people believe in multiple gods. Brahma, Vishnu and Shiva are considered to be the supreme deities – the Creator, Preserver and Destroyer, and together form the Holy Trinity. Ram and Krishna are supposed to be incarnations of Vishnu, and one of the most sacred books of Hinduism is the Bhagavad Gita, which is a compilation of the verses Lord Krishna uttered during the mythological war of Mahabharata to the warrior, Prince Arjuna.

Hinduism is widely followed in India and has deep roots in the country. Popular holidays in India revolve around various Hindu festivals and these are joyous occasions. But religion occasionally becomes a political issue. I am against politicizing religion and believe that it is an individual's personal choice whether they want to practise it or not or if they want to adopt a new faith. According to me, becoming fanatical about your beliefs is a big no.

There are temples in every part of India and many *pandits*, Hindu sages, offer prayers across temples in the country. India's population is Hindu-dominated. People often pray to Indra, the lord of weather, in anticipation of better monsoons, and there are various such practices all across the country. Some of the temples, like the Tirupati Balaji in the state of Andhra Pradesh, have become extremely rich after donations from devotees, and the regular queue to reach the idol exceeds eight hours at times, starting early in the morning and continuing until late.

In the state of Maharashtra, the popular culture glorifies the elephant God, Ganesha, also known as Ganpati. During the festival of Ganesh Chaturthi, people bring home an idol of Ganpati, worship it for a set number of days and then submerge it in the nearest water body or in a bucket in their homes as a symbolic gesture. This festival is widely celebrated, and with greater environmental awareness nowadays, there are eco-friendly idols available. A similar festival is that of Durga Puja in West Bengal, wherein the goddess Durga is worshipped, after which the idols are submerged.

Diwali is another widely celebrated and auspicious Hindu festival and signifies the triumphant return of Lord Ram to his kingdom of Ayodhya after fourteen years in exile, during which he defeated the demon king Ravana. Diwali is celebrated by lighting lamps and burning fireworks. This is progressively reducing due to awareness about pollution and the government's inclination to put a curb on firecrackers as a result. Diwali is also the beginning of a new year in the Hindu calendar.

Holi is another famous festival. Just as Diwali is known to be the festival of lights, Holi is known as the festival of colours and celebrates the victory of good over evil.

Overall, the religious sentiments of the people of India have long been exploited for political gain, and we are now seeing the consequences of this, as the media and the average citizen are waking up to this fact. People have to be tolerant of what others believe in and not engage in acts of violence. I have seen an old friend turn from Hindu to Muslim at a very young age. I stand for this liberal attitude towards worship. A person's choices and beliefs should not be coerced by individuals or the State.

062 | What are the similarities between Jainism and Buddhism?

Jainism and Buddhism both originated in India. While there are some differences between the two religions, their basic principles are the same. Buddhism spread far and wide, such that seven per cent of the global population today is estimated to be practising the faith. Jainism did not spread as widely, and there are comparatively fewer Jains in the world. Lord Mahavira preached Jainism while Lord Gautama Buddha laid down the edicts of Buddhism.

One of the main principles of the two religions is the belief in life after death and reincarnation. Both religions believe that a soul traverses many births until it's purified enough to reach the state of 'moksha', which means freedom from the cycle of life and death upon attaining complete enlightenment. This can occur only after negative 'karma' has been discarded. Good deeds along with penance are the way to attain 'nirvana' during the course of one's life or 'moksha' upon letting go of life within.

According to the two faiths, experiencing hardship and doing meditation are the only ways to reach a higher state of mind and shed the layers of worldliness to purify the soul. Both these religions are known to have been founded before Christianity, and the teachings have been passed down through generations to reach us.

063 | How does one deal with the past baggage of colonialism?

Europe, historically, has been an epicentre of many changes in human history. The Renaissance spanning from the fourteenth to the seventeenth century and the Industrial Revolution of the eighteenth and nineteenth centuries both occurred in Europe. These countries have seen historical glory which is second to none. Their desire to expand their kingdoms and gain more power, access resources, markets and distant geographies led them to set out to different parts of the world, where they established rule. They became increasingly powerful, and the hunger for power drove them out in search of new lands. It is said that at one point, the sun never set on the British Empire.

Almost all parts of the world were ruled by one or other European country. Was that bad for the colonized countries? There is no easy answer to that question. No doubt, the colonies faced economic exploitation, slave trading, dumping of European goods, lack of freedom of people and most of all, lack of autonomy, which the people of the colonized nations craved. Thus, colonies across the globe broke the shackles of foreign rule and set themselves free. However, I think that there were some positives to colonial rule too.

What were these benefits? India was ruled by the British Empire for close to two centuries, and I believe there should be a fair analysis of this period. Europe contributed some amount of infrastructure, such as roads and railways; access to global languages such as French, Spanish and English, law, education, technologies of the Industrial Revolution, literature, culture, architecture, institutions and so on. Most importantly, colonial rule unified these countries into one Commonwealth. Though this was an indirect consequence of colonialism, it is a by-product of this chapter in history. These are some positive takeaways from an otherwise dark period.

The history we are taught in school varies from nation to nation, as the perspective of that country's government is reflected in their textbooks. As there are two sides to a coin, I believe we should see history from a neutral perspective rather than developing antagonistic feelings towards a particular country. For the other country too, some things could be a matter of shame, historically speaking, and it would be unfair to hold the present population accountable for the atrocities committed by people who are long gone. People need to move on from the sentiment and rhetoric of a grudge.

Some erstwhile colonies of Great Britain continue to be part of the Commonwealth, representing our connection with history and our acceptance of the past. Australia and New Zealand carry a version of the Union Jack in their national flags as a kind of symbol.

Today, colonialism in any part of the world is impossible due to the presence of the United Nations, free media and geopolitical alliances. Overall, I am glad colonization is a closed chapter of history, but the takeaways are our gifts and lessons learnt.

Another point to note is that the glorification of freedom fighters shouldn't be viewed as harbouring negative sentiments towards the former colonizers. Freedom was always important to the colonies, so freedom fighters will continue to be heralded as heroes.

064 | Why should you give back to society?

When you measure the qualities of a human being, you can get an idea of what they do for others. Giving doesn't necessarily mean distributing money. It simply means helping the needy, teaching them or giving them the tools to survive and rise up so that they can become independent in fulfilling their needs in the future.

I think engaging in charity and promoting public welfare are very important and should be taken up by all who can, in order to create a better planet. A healthy and happy earth is going to look after our future generations. What good is an excess of money if people are dying of malnutrition or curable diseases?

One significant step in this direction is to pay taxes instead of trying to evade them. Another virtuous venture is to promote clean and green activities and of course, creating value and employment. These are the metrics through which I evaluate businesses and hope I can pass on the passion and fever to others. Encouraging education can make people self-sufficient and they can, in turn, influence others. It starts with a small step and every effort is a stride in the right direction.

Our Enso Foundation, where I am a trustee, is our attempt to make a positive difference in society. It's fulfilling to write a cheque every time I do it. There is no shame in sticking to your financial capacity while donating and every contribution matters. A human wave can start with a single person's attitude.

065| How dirty is politics sometimes?

Vote bank politics is dirty business! I have closely followed many election campaigns and have realized that an immense amount of filth is slung by the leaders of different parties at each other, simply to put down one another. This is not healthy. I am particularly impressed by the British, who maintain politeness and debate with class and dignity. I do not know about other European countries since I don't understand their language, but American and Indian elections are outright mucky. British elections, at least, possess a touch of grace.

India is a land of diversity. Various political parties gain seats in the central government. Two major alliances dominate national politics – the National Democratic Alliance (NDA), which is led by the Bharatiya Janata Party (BJP), and the United Progressive Alliance (UPA), which is led by the Indian National Congress (INC). Thus, the BJP and INC are the two major parties in the country, and their leaders are constantly slinging mud at each other. In everyday conversations, smart people can filter out the truth from the rhetoric, but the common man often falls for the lies that are being thrown around. More often than not, the ruling party is held to be in the wrong and their actions are questioned. Conversely, the opposition is harassed by the party in power, which is often reciprocated when the tables are turned.

Another party in India, the Aam Aadmi Party (AAP), has a strong anti-corruption appeal and a forensic way of working at the grassroots. All in all, healthy debates keep democracy alive, but non-constructive remarks often waste time and pollute the atmosphere.

People need to analyse the role of a national leader and learn to give credit where it is due. I believe we have had some exceptional leaders in the recent past, and they deserve our appreciation for their magnificent work in the challenging position of ruling this country.

To be frank, if I want to make a difference in India, I would do it from a corporate *avatar* and enter politics only through the Upper House or Rajya Sabha. It is extremely tough, and your lifelong reputation could be on the line. The polarization of news channels is an unnecessary evil that all politicians have to deal with. The issue of religious minorities who feel neglected if not addressed constantly crops up and draws media attention.

India being the world's largest democracy, such incidents are bound to happen as people contest for power, and managing them poses a significant task. There are right-wing parties, left-wing parties and parties that are centrists. Personally, I prefer the middle path.

American elections have been no less eventful in any way. Election campaigns take up so much time for the ruling presidents during their second term that one wonders when they manage to perform their duties. Observing the election campaign of Barack Obama and John McCain was a treat, especially considering the USA was in recession.Obama provided the hope and clarity that Americans sought. He was articulate and politically correct, and people knew he was going to win. However, the 2016 elections between

Hillary Clinton and Donald Trump were mucky and people expected a close race, which it indeed was. People opted for Trump and his vision for the USA.

With the media being such a strong fraternity, there are television debates that are outright animalistic, with people howling at each other! Learn from the Brits, I say again, as their manners are truly impeccable. At times, Indian parliamentary sessions are halted due to the commotion, which is detrimental to the democratic process. Debates should be held with decorum, especially within such an esteemed institution, where the nation and world are closely watching.

In politics, people often forget that they have to work on meagre means. Sometimes, individuals enter politics to make dirty money. This holds true for countries where corruption levels are high. While China, being communist, is perceived to have an advantage in this regard, I personally wouldn't want anything less than an improved version of democracy in India, a vision I believe will emerge soon. We are already witnessing change. The people must have a say in the government, and neither communism nor a monarchy align with my concept of an ideal mode of governance.

To appease voters, at times politicians have to lie about their true feelings about a particular issue or abstain from talking about it. Being in the public gaze demands one to be diplomatic at all times, and it often appears that those who seek to gain power do actually hold a mandate for the nation. At least the right ones do, and they aim to translate their vision into reality. I respect such politicians and leaders.

Election manifestos from every political party contain many promises. Leadership styles may vary, but what is important is whether they deliver on the promises they have made. For example, while Dr Manmohan Singh may have been less vocal about issues, Narendra Modi is vocal and participative.

Social media has changed the political landscape to a large degree. People can now interact with their leaders directly. Thus, almost all leaders have clear and articulate views on issues, and the exchange on these platforms can be transformative.

One fundamental action that common citizens and laymen can take is to vote for their candidate; a right, duty and power bestowed upon us by the democratic system. Encouraging others to vote is another way we can contribute, guided by our sense of civic duty. I really admire Arvind Kejriwal, whose anti-corruption drive has instilled fear among the corrupt businessmen nationwide, making them more watchful of their actions. Anna Hazare, Kejriwal's former collaborator, stayed away from politics but led a short yet powerful movement against corruption, offering hope to a billion Indians. Kejriwal has formed the Aam Aadmi Party (AAP) which shows promise to become the third major Indian party.

Politics is dubious, but if things are done in the right way, it is a massive service to the nation! Dirty politics is a waste of time.

066| What is the role of movies in our lives?

I am old school. I like my music with good lyrics and slow, meaningful songs. While music is becoming fast-paced and what I think is 'gibberish', my all-time favourite songs are still by Backstreet Boys, Boyzone, Bryan Adams and Roxette. I like soft rock and occasionally enjoy Hindi romantic music from the nineties and some classics that are even older. I don't enjoy the vulgarity apparent in some modern songs either. I think it's quite passé.

I watch both Hindi and English movies and find that cinema has really evolved to cover a wide range of topics. Films have become far more entertaining than before. The improved visuals and the enhanced sound in theatres and multiplexes have made the movie experience way better than it used to be. OTT platforms allows us to watch almost all old and modern movies at home. Life has become easier from the times of illegal downloads, DVDs, laser disks and cassettes.

In India, movies have always mostly been about love stories but today, a variety of plots can be seen. I find the random song and dance sequences in Indian movies a bit silly. However, some of the contemporary movies are outright amazing and show an outstanding translation of ideas to the screen by filmmakers. It truly is an art to act in and to make movies.

Hollywood movies are sometimes very stimulating too, with a wide range of subjects. They have always maintained a versatile range of genres, which makes the experience enjoyable.

Films and music are made in many countries and in various languages, but those created in the English language continue to have the highest sales. My ideal choice would be to watch dubbed versions of films representing different cultures reaching international shores. Movies can be the bridge connecting all cultures.

Sexually explicit content on screen, which is much more common sight in foreign movies, is not permitted by Indian cinema laws. Audiences emulate movie stars from a young age, so cinema has a much deeper impact on people's minds than one would imagine. Healthy physiques, a fashion sense and lifestyle standards have been set by the movies we watch to a large extent. Fanfare over movie stars is such that people come in hordes to see them.

Objectification of certain sections of society, in films around the world, is a phenomenon should be discouraged instead of emulated. Physical aesthetics and fitness are earned by hardwork, steroids and cosmetic surgeries, but certain aspects of the latter can be misleading for the general public and be proclaimed as unhealthy.

LIFESTYLE

067| How important is it to work out?

It was after my tenth-grade board exams in 2001. I was fifteen at the time and suffered from a lack of confidence. That was when I picked up weights for the first time at the gym in my building complex in Mumbai. Since then, I have never looked back. I began working out religiously and passionately, and slowly, my life changed. My muscles gained definition and my addiction with exercise grew. Everywhere I went, the first thing I would look for was a gym. I went to college in 2003 and there too, I would workout at the college gym. After the first year, I decided to move out of campus into my own apartment and bought weights, a bench and other supplementary equipment online.

Today I am 33 and workout with the same passion. My father too has picked up the habit, and he feels that his day goes on wonderfully after an hour at the gym, which includes some cardio followed by weights. To be frank, muscle-building is a long and tedious process, but once you start seeing results, it doesn't seem like an uphill task anymore. Daily workout then becomes a pleasure. You have to also eat healthy along with workouts to see the best results. The key lies in consistency.

I strongly suggest taking the help of the gym instructor or getting a personal trainer to watch over your form, as that has a huge impact on the effectiveness of your exercise. To get cuts, you also need to do a lot of cardio, that involves cycling, elliptical or treadmill, to burn the fat.

Whenever I have had a long pause in my workouts, I resort to circuit training, which targets each body part. However, on most days, I do focus on two complementing body parts. While exercising the chest, your triceps get worked on too, so I do chest and triceps together. Another such set is the back and the biceps. The shoulder and legs have no connection, but that is the third on the wheel, and then I return to the first combination. My favourite body part to work on is the chest and I do exercises for the abdominal muscles (or abs) every day, lower, upper and lateral.

If you have never worked out before, try it for six months, and your life can change. People who work out have a different air of confidence and higher cognitive abilities. The hormones secreted during workouts also affect your mood. Exercising is recommended for all age groups, but if you have any serious injuries, you must consult a doctor before picking up heavy weights. You must stretch before and after the workout so as to avoid soreness the next day. One must also conduct deep tissue massages once in a while to remove the stiffness caused by exercising. Once your definition is built, it stays for years, a phenomenon caused by what they call 'muscle memory'. It is a safe and long-term investment.

Body metabolism slows down after a certain age and use of concentrated protein supplements must be avoided after a point. I remember trying creatin with whey protein after reaching what I thought was my best form, and soon realized it was not for me. There is ample written material available on the internet about the pros and cons of such formulae.

068 | Are yoga and meditation India's best offering to the West so far?

While the gym helps you gain muscles, flexibility is not addressed. There is also the aspect of working out your mind. Yoga and meditation can be perfect to address these two aspects. Usually, the two can be done together.

Yoga is an ancient Indian art. Plenty of instructors are available today, so be sure to look them up on the internet or find them through references. In recognition of the health effects of yoga, 21 June has been declared the International Day of Yoga by the United Nations General Assembly.

Yoga includes plenty of stretching exercises as well as breathing-focused exercises, categorized as *pranayama*. Yogic exercises include a little bit of breathing-focused meditation as well. Otherwise, focusing on your forehead *chakra* and imagining different colours is a traditional technique that can help calm you down. This is called *preksha dhyan*. The forehead is the location of our pituitary gland, which is the master gland that controls the endocrine system, comprising all glands that secrete hormones. Meditation makes you go deeper into yourself and your mind, and you can learn meditation techniques from numerous centres all over the world that are built to help people experience this wonderful art.

These days, with the help of YouTube videos, one can meditate or learn yoga. For meditation, there are videos with various calming sound effects available. Yoga also offers a lot of exercises for strength building, both inner and outer, and you can learn these exercises by watching videos as well.

Investing in health is very important. They say health is the ultimate wealth. Along with the gym, you should also take up yoga and meditation. Be very careful with some exercises and practise them with caution or under supervision, as you might injure yourself. The best approach is to progress gradually and challenge yourself further and further as you get the hang of it. Getting a trainer or attending a class is recommended. Yoga, indeed, is India's best offering to the world.

069| Do sports help you in other spheres of life?

The only sport I follow religiously is cricket. Cricket comes in three forms, the shortest and the most recent form being the T20, or twenty overs each side. The sport has evolved owing to the large population that follows it. I play cricket; I also played football regularly at one point, although I am an extremely bad player. I have also played tennis as a youngster and represented Delhi state in an under-15 open tournament, clearing just one round in a walk-over and losing to someone younger than me from Karnataka. I have played squash recreationally, finding it the best for fitness, as it requires quick reflexes and fast sprinting. I can just about play badminton and table tennis. I swim once in a while, and find the sport amazing and refreshing. I have played golf a few times – I am not that good at it but I loved the experience. I don't think golf is great for fitness, but it's a relaxant. I jog once in a while, running alongside Mumbai's sea, taking in the fresh air on the most popular road in the city, Marine Drive. It is 3 kilometres long. I am lucky to have engaged in multiple sports from a young age as my parents encouraged it.

Although I studied in the United States, I did not pick up any local sports there. I don't know the rules of baseball, rugby or ice hockey and have played basketball only a few times.

The most followed sport in the world is football. I often feel lost when my friends watch club football, as I am unaware of the different teams and can't decide whom to support. Football requires fitness and I have often been a goalkeeper while playing with my friends,and gotten scorned for being so bad at it.

I strongly feel that sports bind people of different nationalities together. I love to watch cricket, and there was a time when I would adjust my sleep cycle to watch the games taking place in different time zones. In India, although the national game is hockey, cricket is a religion, and cricketers are national heroes. The Cricket World Cup, which takes place every four years, is a time when the productivity of Indians drops (from personal experience) and everyone is actively engaged in supporting the country instead. I can say with some confidence that, in the absence of a quality international football team, it is the biggest sport of the Indian subcontinent. There are cricket stadiums in almost all major cities of India.

More and more nations are beginning to form cricket teams, and now there's also a structured women's cricket league. I am very happy with the way the International Cricket Council (ICC) is handling, developing and nurturing the sport.

I once attended the Wimbledon final in London and a Davis Cup match in New Delhi and didn't find tennis as exciting. Cricket games last longer, but are much more fun to watch. Even playing the sport is so enjoyable; I am a batsman and a fast bowler.

Sachin Tendulkar was sixteen when he began playing for India, and I dearly miss seeing him play after his retirement.

His humility was an inspiration. However, the likes of Virat Kohli and Rohit Sharma have well compensated for his absence. Mahendra Singh Dhoni's coolness is something I try to emulate in my life. He was one of the greatest captains of the Indian cricket team who left a dent on Indian cricket by propelling the game towards higher standards. Rohit Sharma too has won us many a series.

For people with busy work and/or family lives, I highly recommend following and even playing some sport and, more importantly, developing a sporting culture. This habit can go a long way in forming character while keeping you entertained. Sports teach you teamwork and a really fun way to live life. Any sport teaches you to keep your spirits up when faced with loss and to appreciate effort and skill.

070 | Are pets everyone's cup of tea?

Having a pet can be a lot of fun. Cats and dogs can be loving creatures and seamlessly become family members. It is very easy to develop deep emotional bonds with your pets. I had a dog, a golden retriever, whom I named Simba. He died of a snake bite at a farmhouse near Mumbai, and I dearly miss him.

Some people also keep birds as pets, which is something I don't support, because I think caging a living being is cruel. I have bought and set many birds free on the occasion of the Indian Independence Day and felt great about it. I love watching them fly to freedom.

Pets need to be looked after just like little children. They need to be vaccinated, given proper medical treatment when ill, fed nutritious food and be trained. Animals don't possess the intelligence of human beings, but they can be quite clever and very emotional. Some pets recognize their owners immediately, even after months and years of not seeing them. Lately there has been a boom in the number of veterinary hospitals, pet shops and grooming centres. However, it would be wise to nosedive into pet ownership fully knowing the extent of commitment required.

071 | Which way is the global tourism force going?

My first trip abroad was in 1994, when I was nine years old. We covered almost all of Europe, followed by some major cities of the USA, in one summer. It was hectic for the younger me. It was an eye opener for me, and I still remember the theme parks of Orlando, the miniature Amsterdam, the Kohinoor diamond at the Tower of London, the World Trade Centre (which no longer exists) and the Niagara Falls outside Buffalo. Over the years, I have travelled quite a bit and can say with some confidence that I have seen a few countries and cities properly. I have lived in the United States, the United Kingdom and the United Arab Emirates for a considerable period of time. When I compare life outside India to life in India, weighing the pros and cons, I prefer India, and this is largely due to the homely feeling I get in Mumbai, leaving aside the luxury of having house help and drivers.

There was a time when only a few people from India went abroad to study. Today, that number is much higher as more and more people make this choice. As a result, young people end up living overseas more frequently than before. The number of flights has increased, and social media is full of lucrative options for people to go out and explore. Movies today are filmed internationally, thereby exposing the masses to different countries and continents and they, in turn, feel inspired to see the world. Cinema has played a major role in boosting tourism, be it Hollywood, Bollywood or any other film industry.

A lot of countries are minimizing the hassles of obtaining a visa, thus inviting more tourists to their countries. They also give out long-term visas to ease frequent travel. Some countries have recently formed treaties for handing out visas on arrival. I am happy about the step Qatar has recently taken to boost its tourism, where it now provides visas on arrival for citizens from as many as eighty countries. One of the most powerful passports is Japan's as they have no requirement for visa application or visa-on-arrival on travel in over 190 countries. The UAE comes next. This is due to their low tolerance for crime, which makes most countries in the world comfortable to allow their citizens access. The European Union (EU), in my view, is making a mistake in the case of the duration of visas they give. Because these visas are so brief, they are deterring business and tourism opportunities. I am sure they will realize that soon. The USA and the UK both now give ten-year-long visas in some circumstances. Singapore and Dubai are popular destinations for shopping and in terms of activities for children, and both have the option for electronic visas.

One of the most beautiful continents is Europe, with the right mix of nature and historical architecture. You could just get lost in the beauty of the cities there.

The safety index plays a large role in the case of a tourism boost. India has recently made it possible to obtain a visa on arrival at many countries under the leadership of our visionary Prime Minister Narendra Modi, and suddenly the number of Indian tourists in foreign locations has increased dramatically. Even more foreigners come to experience the famous Indian hospitality.

I feel that history adds immense culture and soft power for tourism. India has old forts, palaces, museums with artefacts, temples and natural beauty, all of which are amazing for driving tourism. Work is being done on developing better infrastructure, easing travel and lowering crime rates; the results are visible slowly but steadily.

There are two kinds of locations people most like if they simply want to relax – mountains or beaches. India has both, and although the Maldives has been my favourite vacation spot to date, I have been to Goa frequently and it remains on the top of my list. Another great country to visit, for an amazing experience, is South Africa. There is also Kenya, which is great for safaris, and Tanzania for mountaineering and hiking. Sun City in South Africa is an attraction too, as is Aamby Valley near Mumbai, both man-made spots brimming with activities.

I think I have been to twenty-seven countries in total, which is nothing compared to some of my family members. I am actually a laid-back person and enjoy going to one location and relaxing rather than visiting multiple places and actively sightseeing. Rome is still high on my list, as I am a fan of history and am eager to visit the Vatican (especially after reading Dan Brown's books), but I would rather just laze around. Other places on my bucket list are Hawaii and Australia, in that order.

Sex tourism is being promoted by some governments to increase tourism revenue. I feel like that is going too low, and careful thought must be given to the fabric of culture and upbringing of children in such countries.

Social media along with increase in per capita income globally have resulted in a severe boost in global tourism in the last two decades and we are now witnessing a transformation in tourism trends.

FUTURISTIC TRENDS

072 | How did the invention of the internet change the world?

In the early days of humanity, there was a time when there was nothing to write on or with. Gradually, early human beings began carving inscriptions on stones, which was later followed by writing on leaves. Eventually, paper and the pen were invented, and this was followed by typewriters. Now we have computers.

Computers are a relatively recent invention, emerging in the 20th century. With computers came encyclopaedias such as Microsoft Encarta, providing vast information and distributed in CD-ROM format. However, these resources became obsolete, thanks to a brilliant invention in 1989 by Britain's Tim Berners-Lee, an alumnus of Oxford University. This path-breaking disruption transformed nearly everything that reached our senses. It was the internet, the World Wide Web.

A majority portion of my learning in and after college has been from the internet. Google, Wikipedia, resourceful handles on social media, news websites – you name it. Today, the internet stands as the most powerful tool, offering an infinite knowledge base, accessible simply through our phones, not to mention tablet computers, laptops and PCs. Artificial intelligence is simplifying searching on the internet even further. The future is bright, and upcoming generations are going to be even better at data mining as they will operate these tools from their early years in school. At a young age, they will gain knowledge surpassing that of research scientists from previous years, making them smarter and more aware.

Today, there are websites offering in-depth statistics and data, open-source and closed-source online encyclopaedias, multiple websites and unlimited news reports covering any topic we might want or need to explore. Search engines are the optimal source to dig for information, subsequently transferable to forecasts and in-depth research and analysis. The internet has revolutionized the way we acquire knowledge and empowered individuals to be more resourceful and informed.

073 | How have social media applications become knowledge platforms?

Today the world is smaller than it has ever been before. Even Thomas Friedman could not have envisaged how flat it is in reality.

Imagine a melting pot of human thoughts and emotions being churned and refined on social media platforms like Twitter, Facebook or LinkedIn. Mix in global media, let it sit over time and you have a wonderful content snack ready for your consumption. Nowadays, this is exactly what is easily available, making people infinitely smarter than ever before.

One and a half decades ago came Facebook. It began as a small site for college students and then expanded its reach both geographically and demographically. Nearly everyone across the globe is now a member of the site, providing uninhibited access to pages and information for gathering knowledge. Photos and videos enhance the experience, making it more exciting and entertaining, along with other features designed to enhance the browsing experience on the site. The rapid growth in its popularity is nothing short of incredible.

Let's talk about another site. Who are the smartest and the most influential people on Earth? Who do people want to talk to? We are talking about Twitter, a platform that provides the common population with an opportunity to interact with the who's who. It is a platform where people can learn first-hand about what is happening in the world, obtaining news straight from the horse's mouth and from the trendsetters themselves. LinkedIn also serves its purpose, with its members and content being more serious, whereas Twitter is more interactive and centred around the exchange of ideas. Even the media picks up material from this site.

The real reason for engaging with the brightest minds is to learn from them and be inspired. On Twitter, one can find concrete and actionable statements from leaders and achievers worldwide. People express themselves authentically, enabling others to perceive their aura, personality, lifestyle, interests and much more.

Twitter serves as a valuable platform for the dissemination of information, empowering people who were previously uninformed and relied on minimal news to witness firsthand how trends are set, understand diverse perspectives and find inspiration to achieve their goals. This effect percolates down to the least informed person, showcasing the power of today's social media. Overall, people are way more capable than ever before, and also more knowledgeable.

Listening to celebrities and famous figures discuss real-world issues has made the common man rise up. Mass media and social media today go hand in hand, leading to significant shifts in perspectives across borders and cultures. Thanks to technological improvements, it's all in your palm now. It's a lot of fun too. That fact makes the engagement a symbiotic ecosystem, a world within a world, a microcosm.

074| What is One World?

In this era of globalization, we need to set our sight on goals that were once beyond our reach. With social media, smartphones, the internet and path-breaking technologies, the world has become much smaller, bringing people so close that we are able to overcome the boundaries that used to define us. We are headed towards 'One World'.

Imagine a scenario where international travel requires no visas, everyone uses a shared currency and speaks a common language, such as the dollar and English. People here have no creed, colour, cultural or linguistic divide and everyone enjoys equal opportunities. In this vision, the UN would function as a democratic body, and all economic barriers would have been overcome to make this a reality. This isn't merely scenario planning, rather something I believe we can achieve in reality.

One place where this has worked is in Europe, where the EU is doing precisely that. They have a common currency too, the Euro, trade barriers have been broken down and everyone is involved in lifting others up.

If we can dream of it, it can be realized. With a little compromise and pragmatism, we can embrace each other. This could end the arms race, eliminate two-way trade tariffs and bring about numerous other positive changes. We could put an end to a world so divided that each time we achieve peace, a terror attack or threat of a war looms over us. There is always someone dissatisfied with the status quo.

075 | Does social media motivate us to do better in our life and career?

Social media began in the early 2000s, but the first major success was Facebook, which launched in colleges in the year 2004. I think the world has come a long way since then. Twitter, Facebook, LinkedIn, etc. are great platforms for people to connect and share their experiences, both personal and professional.

There was a time not so long ago when people didn't know how far along in their careers their classmates had gone or what they were currently engaged in. They might have not even known about their marital status after college. With the advent of the internet and social media, we can see what others are doing in real time, and we can know whether they are married, how many children they have and so on. People often post their travel pictures for others to see.

I think this has caused an underlying sense of competition amongst people on social media. Who went to a better school or college? Who got married earlier and who had more children? Who is working in the best firm? All this information is readily available, including when someone gets an offer from a university or a company. Obviously, everyone wants to flaunt their achievements on their profiles and have the best 'trophies' to show off. Looking at the bright side, I think it's wonderful that we are so connected and motivated all the time. However, it can cause social pressure, anxiety and other mental health issues especially as users grow addicted to these platforms. It takes away time from natural life and time that could be used towards constructive activities.

Let's hope people use these sites wisely and take away the best benefits from them. If you are famous, it can also be about who has more followers and that is directly correlated with your fame, importance and likeability.

Thumbs up to social media, but people should be aware of the risks that it comes with: too much use can curb productivity in the workplace. Cybercrimes and stalking should be kept under check, and one must stay alert. Too much of anything isn't good and while I have a company called Enso Webworks that is coming up with its own website, I would like to put a disclaimer on time wastage on all leisure websites such as the social media sites.

076| What could future passports look like?

Barcodes and the electronic chips in credit, debit and various access cards, radio-frequency identification (RFID), etc., have tremendous scope for an increase in the amount of data they can hold. More importantly, they need to be installed with the right code so that the machine scanning them can extract the corresponding data from a centralized server.

During my stint at Oxford University, I attended a lecture on 'scenario planning'. The phrase refers to the ability to imagine and foresee the future and come up with solutions to those issues, in the relevant context. It also opens your eyes to things that could happen or ideas that, if implemented, could change the world.

The United Nations is a global central body, and any initiative they take up can be applied across the world. My prediction is that, just like nanotechnology has shrunk computers, cumbersome passport booklets will shrink to a card that we can keep in our wallets. When we apply for a visa, it will just be uploaded against our name in the central server. And when it's scanned at immigration, our entry in the country will be recorded. While this may sound simple, it is yet not done anywhere in the world today. For ease, the old booklets could go on alongside the new system till such time as the transition to the new system is complete.

Passport booklets are made of paper, and you often run

out of pages when you travel frequently. A card could take care of this problem. The card could store exactly the same amount of information in electronic form as the booklet, and there would be enough space on it to display all necessary information.

The future of passports is definitely a shrunken, electronic version!

077 | How fast is technology evolving?

There was a time when people used oil lamps to light up their houses at night. Soon came Thomas Edison's invention of electric power, and things began to change. Not long after, cars were invented, and following that the Wright brothers invented aeroplanes.

Technological products are being invented since time immemorial. Coal-, oil- and gas-based power generation was used for running electricity power plants, locomotives and vehicles. They were slow and time-consuming. Today, we have much more efficient nuclear power plants, bullet trains and self-driving cars that run on electricity.

When Alexander Graham Bell invented telephones, they were equipped with slow round dials. Now we have smartphones that are not only used for remote conversations, but also to access the internet, either through 5G technology or a Wi-fi connection. Round-dial phones gradually progressed to button-based numerals, and then came cordless phones. There also came about satellite phones, which were used for defence and military purposes, and that technology was later developed into mobile phones, using satellites and towers. Early mobile phones were large and had limited features – they could only be used for talking. Then came SMSs, followed by MMSs, and then finally came the next-generation Blackberries and other palm pilots that could do more than that. Pagers made an entry in the middle of this but were made redundant by improvements in cell phone technologies. Various companies created touchscreen phones with multiple technologies, and their zest for staying ahead of the curve shows, as each model is an improvement over the previous one, be it in terms of speed, memory, functionality or camera quality. Today, the world is connected thanks to these technologies and we can be very grateful to be living in this era where high-tech research is yielding products available at an affordable price, and that have changed the way we do almost anything. Many companies such as Samsung, Google and Nokia have followed suit after Apple's mass-market breakthrough, and are now manufacturing their own versions of smartphones. I personally like Apple iPhones the best.

Cell phones are not the only things that have evolved. Think about early cars, their speed and manual gearboxes, and compare them with today's sleeker models, which run much more smoothly, have GPS navigation and are even automated, often through touchscreen panels. Who knows if one day we will look back and say these products are inferior to what we have then? It might happen, but they are still cutting edge compared to what the previous generations had. Driverless cars are already in action in Pittsburgh, Pennsylvania in the US as well as in many other cities around the world.

In terms of air travel, travel times are decreasing and direct flying distances are increasing. Planes like Concorde by Airbus could fly at double the speed of a normal aircraft, but that has been made redundant due to safety issues. Research is still ongoing for building faster aircrafts. Boeing and Airbus have always been competing against each other for the majority of the aircraft market, followed by Bombardier,

Sukhoi, Gulfstream and many others. We have the mighty Airbus A380, which has two storeys inside its cabin and can cover huge distances. Wi-fi is now available on planes, and we can soon anticipate cell phone signals reaching the sky. Live TV channels are possible too nowadays.

Earlier, the train travel time between Mumbai and Delhi was about twenty-four hours, but today it's an overnight ride. Bullet trains in Japan, China and other parts of the world travel at incredible speeds. The Hyperloop can take you from point A to B in no time. Japan is the country that has pioneered this technology.

Hence, technology and science are evolving in every sphere. I can go on and on – cable TV, varied websites and mobile apps, banking, e-commerce, defence, medicines, diagnostics. The list is long and never ending. We must remember to never be complacent, as we have to accept changes and improvements as they come and learn to make the most of them. Future generations are going to have computers that are much faster and sleeker than even today's tablets. Well, our cell phones are like computers. At one time, a PC was gigantic, had very little memory and was much slower. Just imagine how far we have come in just two decades, and how far we can go.

The evolution of technology is based on demand and supply, as demand fuels research money invested in products. Today's consumers want everything fast and they want it now. They want it at the right price too. Hence, R&D is continuously ongoing at large corporations, which deliver these products. Their valuations are reaching hundreds of billions of dollars or even crossing a trillion, which goes to show the faith people have in these companies.

In terms of usage, trying to stay ahead of technology is like trying to stay ahead of time, and we have to do that to survive. If we can't operate the latest gadgets, someone who can will make us redundant. Always stay buckled up for something new!

After a point, it's going to the end of inventions as we know them and things like artificial intelligence will take over. Nanotechnology will make products smaller in size and design will be key to determine functionality. This is my prediction. We are at the tipping point of faster precision in technology along with speed, efficiency and cost effectiveness. With rapid industrialization, there is going to be a surge in supply, especially due to the emerging economies that will keep a check on prices. Inflation has been a temporary phenomenon due to the Russia–Ukraine crisis and Covid-19 prior to that.

SUCCESS SECRETS

078| Are good manners essential for success?

One of the most important things in life is graciousness. Nowadays soft skills are taught in B-school curriculums as they have become increasingly important in our real-world transactions. These skills are important for interpersonal communication and help one gain a better standing in society. Your manners can literally make you stand out.

Some people can take so much for granted in their lives – meals, the roof above their head, civic amenities, fundamental rights and much more. But there are many more people who live in dire circumstances without access to some or any of this. Greeting them with a polite smile can be enough to light up their day. I say 'thank you' to all servers all the time, and it has become a part of my manners. I thank the watchman and the lift man, my driver and everyone else who does something to make my life easier. Even my family members get a word of thanks when they check on how I am doing. I feel that with this attitude, I have an edge over others.

How often have you heard people use the words 'sorry' and 'please'? It is like music to the ears when people repeat them, reassuring us that manners still exist. There are many habits that, if followed, can be extremely appealing to the people around you.

Muhammad Ali once said that if someone treats a waiter

at a restaurant badly, he wouldn't trust him, as he would have treated Ali himself badly had he been that waiter. That is wisdom. I am an inspired person, having observed a lot of great minds. One thing all of them have in common is good manners. Humility is attractive. Humble people are appreciated and lauded at every step. It is a must-have quality. In exchange for your good manners, you can get many brownie points from your observers. However, the real reason why you should be polite is for self-satisfaction.

I have witnessed servers being ill-treated in front of me, and only I know how terribly I judged these people and how I wanted to stay away from them thereon. I was highly embarrassed and hoped to never see something like that happen ever again. Remember to keep your feet on the ground and your head held high. To do that, one must showcase exemplary manners.

One should always stand up for the aged and disabled, hold the door open for whoever is behind us, wait and hold the elevator open for the person coming towards it, never jump a queue, never honk while driving, let pedestrians cross first and remember to tip graciously if you are at the receiving end of a service. Good manners help build strong character, which goes a long way in life.

Right from school to adolescence to adult life, we see a diverse lot of people in life. There's the lot that is brash and believes in brawls and rowdy behaviour or those who pass provocative comments. The best way to tackle with them is not to indulge them and to take it up with supervisors; or, if it's outside an institution, you should definitely take it up with law enforcers. There is no point in replying or reacting, as that is what such people feed on. I have gotten into a few brawls at different stages of my life, and each time I have come away with a bad aftertaste. I have even had a bleeding nose once. In my view, just ignore these people and walk away. If you feel threatened, just run to safety. You don't have to feel like you chickened out, rather, feel like you did the more mature thing. There are rotten apples everywhere and their pastime is to harass others. There is little you can do about them, so save your energy for better things.

Your manners should be impeccable, and like the finer things in life, they come free of cost. You can leave a deep impact on someone just with the way you conduct yourself. Always display yourself graciously. Your smile can change someone's day.

079| Are some good habits irreplaceable?

There are many habits that one could follow to make a good impression on others and lead a fulfilling life. Here are a few of them:

- One must focus on being neat and presentable. If you are a man, you must shave regularly. In case you keep stubble, it should be trimmed properly and not be allowed to grow haphazardly. Your nails should not be overgrown, as that looks extremely shabby. It is extremely off-putting when people look unkempt.
- Tipping is a good habit after a meal or a cab ride or for any service. If you can spare the change, it goes a long way.
- A very good habit is reading and following current affairs to stay up to date with what is going on in the world. A person who sounds like they are keeping up with the times leaves a good impression. These days, the news is literally free on social media, and you can choose and pick what you want to read.
- A very good habit is waking up early and sleeping on time. The recommended minimum amount of sleep is seven to eight hours, so you must go to bed early to get plenty of rest and wake up as early as possible. It is said, 'early to bed, early to rise, makes a person healthy, wealthy, and wise', and I do find some truth in this

adage. There is a popular belief in China that people who wake up before sunrise will always do well. The belief originated with the rice farmers, who thought that early risers would never let their families starve. This is definitely true. Early mornings are a quiet time to get things done. Starting work early can be good too, as you can be done with your work early and have the evening to relax. The morning is a time for certain hormonal secretions in the body and if you are awake at that time, you can benefit from it greatly.

- Being on time is another very good habit. People who are late for their commitments often fall behind people who are on time. This is a small secret of greatness that can define you. Your reputation precedes you, and if you are known to be one who takes others' time seriously, you are going places in life.
- A very good habit is not to waste food. If you have extra, find a homeless person and give it to them. Sadly, food is a luxury for some people, and we must appreciate it if we get it easily. It's a habit among me and my friends to pack food after a meal at a restaurant and give it to a homeless person on the way back.
- A good habit is not to intervene when someone is talking and to listen patiently. Listening is an art, and one can learn a lot by listening carefully to others. I find that it is not something everyone does, but we must try. Every person has had varied experiences and has things to say which, if heard, can add to the richness of your knowledge base. Good listeners are better heard too.
- People sometimes don't call others back or miss replying to correspondence. I think that's a bad habit,

and we should always respond to those who reach out to us. I always try to return all calls and messages. No matter how busy you are or how inconsequential the person at the other end is, you must respond – that is the thumb rule.

- Jotting down 'things to do' or 'things to remember' is a particularly good habit, as it makes life easier. You could just strike-through items on the list once completed. It's a great way not to forget anything.
- Among other good habits are exercise, meditation and going for strolls. Staying fit increases mental and physical strength, and you can achieve more in less time, as your efficiency increases.
- Lastly, the worst habit I can think of is throwing garbage anywhere but in dustbins, and spitting in public. Throw trash where it belongs – in bins. It is our job to keep our cities, forests and oceans clean. Treat the world as your home and preserve it for everyone to cherish.

080| What happens without ethics and integrity?

I once cheated in a sixth-grade mathematics exam by copying answers from my friend, who sat in front of me and voluntarily shared his answers. We were caught, and our parents were called to the school. Both my friend and I denied it, and we were let off. Feeling overwhelmed by guilt, I approached the teacher at the end of the episode and professed my mistake, and she let me go with a smile and a warning. This is when we were young. Warren Buffet once stated that mistakes in youth can be erased, but this doesn't hold true in adult life. He observes that this is evident from the fact that we use pencils when young, which can be erased, and pens as we mature, which use permanent ink. So truc.

Ethics form the backbonc of our charactcr, earning a person respect, admiration and a following. Many exploit the system and race ahead of others, but only a few manage to get ahead the right way. Achieving success through any and all means at your disposal may earn you the admiration of others, but it will never command the respect you seek. Only a person with high ethics gains the soft power to be heard and respected.

There is no shortcut to success, and some people, in their quest of get ahead, make mistakes and falter by breaking the law. Some get away with serious crimes and everything ends well for them, but in other cases, individuals are caught, and they never get ahead as they are never trusted again. Their careers are doomed due to their criminal behaviour and unethical conduct, leading to a bleak future.

Ethics are taught in nearly all B-schools as a subject, emphasizing the importance of imbibing ethical principles in our daily conduct and dealings and carrying out our day-to-day work with integrity and honesty. At times you may feel that you can get away with lying, cheating and stealing, but any of these will make you fall in your own and others' eyes, ultimately troubling your conscience and causing sleepless nights.

Be a person of modest means but strong ethical conduct, and you will see that you are happier. In the long run, those who betray the very sources of validation they seek will suffer the most.

The values instilled by the leaders of an organization or institution play a crucial role in adding to the attractiveness of that entity. Bodies with ethical leaders at the forefront are more likely to do well than others.

081| Is any job too menial?

I was born and brought up in India. Here, labour is cheap, and many people, not just the wealthy, have the privilege of employing domestic help to assist them in their homes. There are chauffeurs available to drive your cars and so on. One valuable lesson my grandfather has taught us is that no job is too small. I remember him teaching me how to wash dishes and sweep the floors when I was a child. In doing so, we learned to empathize with those working for us, fostering kindness and appreciation for their efforts. In some developed economies, almost everyone does these household chores by themselves, and it is a part of their daily routine. While living in the US and later in the UK, I realized that I was comparatively spoilt and couldn't be as independent as the locals, which made me feel weak. I really think that it is important to be able to do all the necessary chores yourself as it gives you a unique sense of empowerment.

Bill Gates has expressed his love for washing his own dishes, Narayana Murthy of India has mentioned cleaning his own toilet sometimes. These are accomplished people who can afford all the help they need. They do this because they feel a need to be grounded and connected to their roots. I second that. Understanding that no job is too small is a vital lesson, regardless of one's status or accomplishments. No job is menial.

082 | Why are role models important?

Since time immemorial, there have always been champions in almost every field, individuals who have mastered their specific areas. In India, cricket is huge with the cricketer Sachin Tendulkar being a true legend of the sport. He is a role model for hundreds of thousands of budding cricketers in India and around the world. His records speak for themselves. Similarly, across the world, singers aspire to be like the legendary Bryan Adams, Celine Dion or Madonna. Actors aspire to be like Morgan Freeman or Tom Hanks and in India, Shah Rukh Khan. For women, the role models are Julia Roberts, Meryl Streep and so on. These achievers have high set standards of mastery in their field for others to follow. There are deceased legends too, like Mahatma Gandhi and Martin Luther King Jr., whose legacies continue to shine for us. I am certain that their unmatched impact on social engineering inspires many aspiring youngsters who want to change the world for the better. Did these great people have role models when they were creating ripples? I am sure they did.

It is not belittling to desire to be like someone else. It is actually humbling. Role models or idols can change over time, but they should be carefully selected. For some people, their own parents serve as role models. That is a good thing. My father has been a role model for me too, but I have multiple individuals I look up to. I look up to Ratan Tata for his outstanding achievements in business. I look up to Bill Gates for his charitable nature and his ability to stay ahead of everyone else for so many years. Both these people have qualities in common – they are champions of the business and philanthropic world, serving as a source of inspiration for one and all.

Idols are always a source of hope. Like the North star, they can guide you from afar.

083 | How many friends can you count on?

Friendship is a profound psychological contract. Relationships are a serious matter, as they are a great source of support in whatever we set out to do in life. If you have someone to talk to about every issue that comes to your mind and have a good adviser and confidant in your buddy or two, you are very lucky.

Relationships begin from your school years, when you have many friends and your issues aren't that serious and neither are relationships. The friendships get deeper as you grow older and there is a polarization of the like-minded ones, or 'common interest groups'. This happens during college, and that is when friendships peak, I feel, as they did for me. As you enter the workplace, you tend to roam around in cliques, and the circles get smaller and smaller with time, leaving you with more meaningful but fewer relations. Working friendships can be fun too, but those that you carry with you from school and college often form your backbone. These are people you can confide in with ease, even after long lapses in communication.

Loyalty is a must in friendships. When trust is broken, it often hurts. Sometimes we may get dumped by friends as we are of no use to them, or friends may change as their need for other people in their life gets more calculative, as does their idea of friends and interests. The best is to be strong and move on, as friendships that really add value are mature, adult bonds that are complete and loyal. True friends are people you should really cherish and value.

A lot of friendships are easy going and don't demand too much. However, some people are very needy and demanding and hold others back. That is not healthy. The best is to guide these people into real-life matters and not to let them affect your career. Don't let friendships become toxic.

Healthy friendships can turn into life-long connections, where your spouses and children also become friends. They can sometimes turn into business partnerships or at least a frequent mutual give and take of ideas, along with guidance and companionship. I strongly believe friends are important, but good friends are more important, and they will always be a close few.

084 | What is the difference between horses and mules?

Have you ever heard of a mule being admired for its hard work? I haven't. People often make fun of them instead and exploit them. However, we admire horses, which are supposed to have higher intelligence than mules. The point I am trying to make is that one has to work smartly, not just put in more hours. I am not at all implying that hours are not important – but those hours should be effective and you need to continuously sharpen your edge.

I strongly believe that people working across all positions, anywhere, adhering to tiring daily routines, must take time out and go on vacations, get enough rest on weekends and make the most of their free time to create a proper work–life balance. Western countries, largely the developed part of the world, have realized this. That is why all shops and businesses there are closed on Saturdays and Sundays. Imagine reaching a point of fatigue where your brain isn't productive because of overload. It is like working with a computer giving continuous errors. And that's a big no, according to me.

We have to spend time with our near and dear ones, get fresh air, exercise, listen to music, watch television, spend time on social media and be up to date with our understanding of current affairs. All that requires setting aside time for ourselves. People must resort to hobbies as they can be very relaxing. Hence, a healthy work–life balance is a must.

085 | Which laws of physics are analogical to human tendencies?

We always prefer to stay stagnant and be comfortable. Today's work happens through palm pilots and tablet PCs, which are conducive to a state of lethargy. Einstein's theory of relativity says that till an object from a state of rest is not given a push, it will stay there. Therefore, we see that we all need to push each other and challenge each other in many forms to go out there and do more.

There is only 1–2 per cent of the human population that makes it to the uppermost economic strata, while the rest remain in a state of inertia all their lives; content, but not reaching the heights that the top 1–2 per cent are at. The difference is that the top tier pushed harder and the others simply didn't care. To each their own, but why just read the news when you can be a newsmaker? Why just sit back and work for someone when you can employ others and do something bigger and better than what you are currently doing? It's all a personal choice, but you must always try to excel in whatever you do.

People often want to be recognized, especially ambitious youngsters. Some want recognition for their fancy degrees, rich parents, a good-looking girlfriend or a fancy car, but what they don't realize is that there are many who aspire like them. At every stage, there will be a new target to be reached and new hurdles in life, as life is designed to challenge you. You have to continuously build on what you have, no matter what stage of life you are at.

The other side of this page is Newton's theory of gravity. Mass attracts mass. I strongly believe that we, as a society, are inter-linked, even more so now through social media. We all impact each other. People from different spheres of life interact on various platforms, and the gravitational attraction between humans is way more than before.

Consequently, a small push can change everything, including the state of equilibrium. If all of us start adding value to each other's lives and pushing everyone to reach newer heights, we can take advantage of these laws of physics to be better versions of ourselves and thus be better producers and consumers. This push is the force that, if it's powerful enough, can break the state of equilibrium and can take moon out of the earth's orbit!

086 | Is reading really as beneficial as it is said to be?

Reading books can be quite relaxing. Ever since I picked up my first book, which was one of the *Famous Five* ones, I haven't stopped reading. I think I have finished all *Famous Fives, Secret Sevens, Hardy Boys* and even *Nancy Drews*, for which I was made fun of in class once. I have read vociferously, and my reading over time has evolved to autobiographies and interesting informational volumes. Among fiction writers, I now like Dan Brown a lot.

Reading is a habit that pays huge dividends, and my maternal grandfather always lectures me on this habit and says that I should never give it up. He is retired, so he has free time, which he spends reading a lot – often two to three newspapers a day and magazines.

I like books that you don't feel like putting down. They are often better even than watching movies. Reading is such a pleasure that, when you have good books with you and time at hand, it just flies. A great way to pass the time.

One of the most distinguished authors of today, Yuval Noah Harari, has written three massive books on human evolution and anthropology. I have read the first one, *Sapiens*. It is informative and Harari's depth of knowledge is immense. Because of its length, however, fatigue builds up after a point. I know people want value for their money, but this is part of the reason I have kept my essays short in this book. I want my readers to enjoy the reading experience.

The availability of reading material today is immense. I often read online, going on Wikipedia, Investopedia and other such websites, or simply by browsing through a search engine like Google to dig for facts and information. It keeps me up to date and, more often than not, I discover something new. That feeling when you have figured out something you have been thinking about for a long time is just amazing, and it's all thanks to the vast knowledge databases on the internet, which are now accessible on our phones. I read most of my news through media Twitter handles and just skim through newspapers.

There is no substitute for reading if you want to keep yourself entertained, learn new things or pass the time well. Be sure to inculcate this habit in your children, as it will take them a long way.

087| Is life a sprint or a marathon?

Sachin Tendulkar is one of India's finest ever products in the field of sports, historically speaking. He set the precedent for successors like Rohit Sharma and Virat Kohli. He was an amazing batsman, and people often lauded him for his good temperament. He would never let the crowd's screams and shouts and his larger-than-life presence get to his head. That's what made him outstanding and allowed him to outperform others.

Life is like a sport with spectators. Like Sachin, you have to stay focused and move ahead towards the finish line without looking at the spectators and not letting them affect you. Once you reach the finish line, you may rest for just enough time before you prepare yourself for the next goal, and this could be further away than the one before. Once you reach there, you have to again look down, not left or right, and get to the next line. Those who can do this reach far in life, as they keep striving higher but stay focused and within their wits. They don't take undue risks. Life is long; it shouldn't be a sprint.

At no point should one let go of one's equanimity. Celebrate just enough so you can get up the next morning and work with focus.

088 | How does one filter noise from facts?

People often think they know it all. It is exhausting to be around someone who thinks their opinions are facts and thus always right. I have had personal experiences with many such people. They have a superiority complex about their knowledge as if it's unique. They are also the most likely to buy into the crazy conspiracy theories out there.

I have been proven wrong many times and I find no shame in admitting it. I politely apologize and change course. I am easy to correct. I find that I become an easier person to connect with that way.

While it's easy to admit your mistake once or twice, to do it multiple times can be demeaning and may require guts. Nevertheless, you should still do it. You can easily say that you are unsure and that particular thing should be verified. By doing that, you automatically fall into the 'nice' category and become someone who everyone wants to associate with. More importantly, your credibility isn't fogged by incorrect facts.

Not only at the workplace, but even elsewhere I have engaged in many debates, where some people are boisterous and loud with their statements, each one thinking that their analysis is the correct one. Sometimes rumours, or supposedly information from higher channels, which are misconstrued, can cause this to happen, and they could be lies too. One must be very careful in today's world in evaluating right against wrong. Do not be a pawn in the bigger game but try to see the underlying currents to know the truth.

Question the facts stated by others. Scan news for noise. Admit when you have been wrong. And lastly, be as high up in the chain of correct information as possible.

Even news media like websites, TV channels, newspapers, magazines and so on can create a layer of ambiguity and noise around us. We have to build our own views gradually and see if we are right, and if there is a solution to a problem or a clear viewpoint. Sometimes, a certain person may have an impact on you while watching a debate on TV news channels, and your views on that particular topic are refined by them. Delve deep into each subject that interests you so that you have the necessary information at your fingertips. The internet is a treasure-trove of information, just waiting to be discovered.

089 | How high should you set your needs?

The basic needs of a human being are constantly increasing. With the advent of online media and social media, today's working person wants more out of life as they have exposure to more. So what should be someone's immediate goals? If you ask any individual, they will all say different things based on their vision of what they can achieve or what they believe is feasible. Let's reflect on some levels of lifestyle that people strive for.

If you ask a farmer in Africa during a bad season, what their basic needs are, they would say it is to simply feed themselves and their families. It is unfortunate how income disparity affects your basic needs.

To take the example of travel, a lot of people travel by buses and trains from one city to another, stay in cheap hotels and use local transit or if they can afford it, the slightly costlier and more comfortable ones. These people aim to travel by air one day and stay in a nicer hotel. Some people haven't travelled much internationally, and they aim to do so with their families. These could be your basic needs in today's world.

The next scale is for people who already travel by air and stay in good hotels, and they usually aim to travel in business class and stay in premium five-star hotels. That is my idea of a comfortable life. I could manage with that. Following that comes staying in larger suites in hotels and flying in first class. That is always nice.

The extremely rich own private jets, which are not affordable for most of the world's population, and there are always those who stay in the presidential suites of hotels.

Some people have house help to do their cleaning and washing and chauffeurs to drive them around. In countries like India, where the minimum wage is very low, loads of people have multiple staff members making life easier for them, but that is a rare luxury in the developed world, as the cost of labour is much higher there. The rich have to spend more on the same luxuries.

Some people never rest. They want bigger jets, more holiday homes abroad and maybe a yacht. There is no limit to their wants and needs. Richard Branson has a private island, Al-Waleed Bin Talal had an Airbus A380 which he later sold. There is a race to own a sports team at times. In India, the annual Indian Premiere League (IPL) for cricket sees corporates and celebrities bid for teams and later own them. People buy soccer teams or sponsor Formula 1 cars. There is so much you can do with money. But if set your needs to 'basic' and then mind map everything that you get above that as a 'bonus', you will appreciate things more.

Each person wants to own a home but some can't afford it. They rent out an apartment and live within modest means. In some cases, their employer provides accommodation. Many people aim to buy their own apartment one day. Then there are those who have their own home or multiple homes in different cities. There are people with one car or multiple cars, basic or premium. There is no end to expectations. The idea of basic needs varies from person to person, but there is no use being unhappy after a certain point. Discontentment arises only when you compare yourself to others. You can live a happy life by just being satisfied. While there is no harm in striving for a better life, that shouldn't be a source of pressure and unhappiness. People often take risks or shortcuts to get wealthier, thereby destroying what they have built. People must be content at some point. Go for organic growth in your career and grow in your needs *proportionately*. Keep basic needs simple. Save enough.

I have a friend in Mumbai who is a classic example of someone who assesses an item's value for money before making a purchase decision, even if he can afford it. That is the right attitude, in my view.

090 | How much can you learn after finishing your final degree?

We begin learning from right after we are born. In school and college we encounter formal, structured education and learn the things we need to function professionally. We learn specific subjects at the college level and acquire skillsw that helps us begin a career. Through our careers, we gain experience, which is a very integral part of the learning curve. And that is a process that must not stop. A curious mind wanders and forever tries to gain knowledge and apply it while analysing different topics. I do that and I find it to be worthwhile.

Something I respect about scholars and academics is their tireless pursuit of knowledge in order to impart it in meaningful and effective ways. People who follow these heroes live a long, productive and content life. I see my father gather information through social media, news and his daily interactions, and I find it inspiring. His curiosity makes him interesting to be around, and one realizes the value of this habit. Your brain constantly needs food for thought, and staying in touch with your curious side is the best way forward, no matter what your age or profession is.

Aside from daily news and documentaries that are excellent sources of knowledge, there are also various university publications that you can access. All universities have social media handles that publicize these publications. You can follow these and obtain in-depth and cutting-edge research, and that too for free. Sometimes you may have to subscribe to get the advanced package, and those are usually worth it. Oxford University Press, Cambridge University Press, Harvard Business Review and MIT Technology Review are all high-quality publications. Reading these is a great way to fuel your mind.

Learning must never stop. There is only so much that formal education can teach you. However, with the help of today's tools, people can learn all their lives and, sometimes, even more than they would have if they were still in university. Teach yourself to learn diligently through various sources, and you will always be interesting to those around you. It is important to do this, as knowledge imparted through formal education becomes outdated periodically.

I was fortunate to have landed at one of the most premier institutes – Carnegie Mellon University. Hence, my computer skills and data mining ability are higher than many others I know.

091| Can we all impact multiple lives?

To do something extraordinary in life, a person needs to understand that each individual has the power to make a change. It can be through something as simple as exercising the right to vote. A person can create ripples by putting forth their ideas in a sound, logical manner. This should be a daily habit as healthy discussions are an excellent means of refining thoughts and connecting with like-minded individuals. Others can join in if they like your ideas and in togetherness you will find the future of your ideas. We have to learn to get over fear, hatred and malice as these differences form boundaries between people. These differences may exist due to religious sentiments or historical situations, but one must shed these and move ahead as a unified voice. This is in everyone's best interest.

Getting others to listen to you is the best way to influence them. You have the most impact if what you are promoting is in everyone's interest and is aligned with a higher cause or the greater good. To be great one doesn't need to be from any specific background– anyone can achieve anything if they put their mind to it. The biggest success stories are people who have come up from the ground up in their field, be it politics, acting, business or sports. These people were supported by many others and they were unified in helping them rise. There is no lone ranger – that's just a state of mind. The reason people help others is simply because they want to see them succeed. Believe it or not, the biggest secret to success is the ability to care for others around you. Your ability to care is reflected in your work, regardless of profession.

Let's take the example of business. Jack Welch led his company to great heights over the course of his career . His dedication to work allowed his company, General Electric, to create change. General Electric was smart and ethical and delivered good products and services which showed care for consumers.

To have an impact on people, you must first become worthy of creating that impact. Everyone possesses the power to make a change but the degree to which this change is effective varies. The more successful you are in your field, the greater the power to influence others. Sometimes, your relevance to the world can be determined by how many lives you affect through direct or indirect means.

092| Should we leave a tip everywhere?

These days, a service charge is often included in the bill along with the meal at a restaurant. My father has taught me one very valuable practice that I follow and that is to leave generous tips for any service. The anticipation of generous tips can be a great incentive for people to take up various positions and excel at them. If you happen to be in a position of privilege and can afford to share some of your good fortune, you should. It is a good deed.

My father's company had an investor in the year 2000 – the late Kerry Packer, who visited Mumbai along with his son James. Before checking out, they left a large tip at the Oberoi hotel, an amount unheard of then. I feel gestures like these show that you care.

I wasn't aware that in New York City people tip at bars too and thus overlooked it. However, a scornful look by one of the staff cleared any confusion I had. A similar situation occurred when I was in London and tipped only a small amount after a cab ride. The driver scoffed at me and I have been careful since then.

Tipping is good manners and an excellent way to thank someone for their service. Interestingly, 'gratuity' has the same etymological root as the word 'gratitude'. It is good practice to be abundantly grateful.

SOCIAL EMPOWERMENT

093 | Is attending prestigious educational institutions crucial for success?

I am an alumnus of three world-class universities – Carnegie Mellon, Oxford and Cambridge – although I dropped out of the last one. I also attended London Business School for an executive education programme. Being an alumnus of such prestigious universities has made me realize how universities have become brands that youngsters wear during the formative years of their careers – a badge made more shiny with the advent of social media.

University rankings can become an important marker in the lives of young people. The U.S. and the UK account for almost all top universities in the world, followed by a few other countries like Australia, Japan and China.

There are two kinds of universities – science-focused and arts-focused. I would say Massachusetts Institute of Technology (MIT), California Institute of Technology, CMU, Cambridge and so on are science-focused universities. Meanwhile Harvard, Oxford, Berkeley and University of Pennsylvania are liberal arts-focused universities. Personally, I like liberal arts-focused universities more as they are more social and fun.

Historically, Indians and Greeks formed the earliest learning institutions in the world. Oxford came about as the earliest university in the English-speaking world. Then Cambridge was created as a result of local unrest and thus became the the second ever university to grace the West. John

Harvard from Emmanuel College at Cambridge University founded Harvard University in Massachusetts in the U.S.

I am lucky to have gone to research-based universities as they allowed me to acquire good-quality education. Such an acquisition is important but it's not everything. The richest men today are college dropouts thus making it quite clear that education can't supersede common sense and other positive personal qualities.

It is true that you need a bit of everything to get ahead in life but it is also true that studying – at any university – with an attitude to gain knowledge is also needed to get ahead. University provides you with an environment that allows you to gain a lot from peer-to-peer interaction and to learn to be independent. It helps with character formation and the qualifications you earn give you a security blanket for life. I personally enjoy studying and consider myself to be a geek. The best thing that happened to me was going to CMU, where I really discovered myself. I would therefore suggest that you use your university experience to form your character and have fun while you're at it.

Another important piece of advice worth mentioning is that one must never be so proud of their educational qualification and academic achievements that they stop listening and learning. You must critically analyse everything and practice empathy. Putting yourself in the shoes of someone you are scrutinizing will help you understand their perspective.

In the case of billionaires that dropped out, let's see what could have caused them to leave their college midway–

1. Their business started making money and they saw a clear road ahead.
2. They were not interested in books.
3. Both.
4. Neither.

What about the ones who did not have a business while they were in college? What could be the reason they got to a certain position in life? Some possible answers could be–

1. They wanted to redeem themselves after the educational failure.
2. They always thought too big and 'out of the books' for academics, and hence, were free-spirited and that helped them.
3. Both.
4. Neither.

These are just speculations but you get the gist of this exercise. There are more people you can analyse and learn about once you delve deeper into their lives. By no means should you drop out of college after reading this book. It becomes difficult to take up formal education once you cross a certain age and you are likely to regret your decision if you do end up dropping out.

People might not think it's easy to understand what made someone like Mahatma Gandhi so great, but those were the days of extreme injustice, and a hero had to rise. Gandhi became this modern-day messiah. Reading his autobiography, you realize that there has to be that passion in a man's soul that unlocks his wisdom to those that seek it, and wisdom is just as important as knowledge.

Rankings can be extremely misleading when it comes to universities. Healthy competition between universities is good but each is a temple of knowledge and learning. Take them seriously, both while studying at them and much after graduating from them.

094 | Which part of society should you give back to?

I am very fond of educational institutions. The ones I attended have given me everything and there is nothing better than teaching people a variety of subjects. I have always maintained that education is a must as it's a lifetime's insurance from problems. Contributing to educational institutions can enable affordable or even free education for many students, thus enhancing their quality of life. One must contribute to the education of the underprivileged by donating to scholarship funds, universities and schools. Various NGOs are also working for child education. Charity is personally fulfilling. Try it.

I don't believe in giving out cash to people as it's better to enable them to earn instead. Everyone should give back to society by donating to charitable trusts, foundations and organizations that are working for the betterment of our future. Donating to any cause close to your heart can help make a difference for them. You should also try to rope in your peers to do the same.

Our foundation has drawn up a long charter where education is a key focus area. Together we can end global problems– hunger, illiteracy, ailments and poverty. Creating a bridge between the rich and poor is the need of the hour, particularly in the developing world, where income disparity is high. Lift everyone up. There is power in collectivism.

095| How does law evolve?

Law is supposed to be blind to any sort of bias. When civilization started, the initial force that led people to settle down and bound them to the right path was probably religion. Religion taught people about right and wrong, good and bad. However, as commerce crept in, religious law was not enough to maintain societal harmony. The evolution of kingdoms led to the emergence of law.

Law is easy to understand if your moral compass is high. The law usually favours what is right in the basic sense. In the complex sense, each and every thing is defined well in the law books and there are usually preceding cases that can be referred to in complex situations. Thus, the law also evolves. The job of the jury is to pass judgment based on the book of law, not on their own personal sense of right and wrong. Loopholes in the law are often exploited and we see amendments being made and deviant cases being quoted periodically, which then set the precedent for the next case on that subject.

Some countries have a common federal legal structure that is applicable to the entire country, while others have separate laws for each state. Law has been a subject very close to my heart, not only because my maternal uncle – who is very close to me – is a lawyer, but also because I study it in my free time. I strongly believe that being ignorant of the law is not an excuse to break it.

Sometimes, law enforcers have no clarity about what they are doing or about citizens' rights, but they should be educated on these subjects. There are two kinds of law – civil and criminal.

The constitution of any country is the ultimate book of law that must be followed. The articles therein are used to enforce law. The direction the law takes on is determined by the constitution, which varies from country to country. For instance, some countries are secular while others are theocratic. In the latter case, the law is affected largely by the predominant religion in that country. Most theocratic countries are Islamic and their laws and constitutions are different from those of secular countries.

Sometimes age-old laws are still applied in many countries, and the process to change laws that might be outdated is through discussion in the parliament. Governments don't review complex processes on a daily basis and only do so when it is needed. Any proposed change needs to be thought out well. Archaic laws that aren't applicable today – as situations have changed – should be done away with. This could help courts in making decisions and save everyone time.

Every citizen of every country must learn as much as possible about the law. It is empowering to do so and leading an aware life gives you an edge over others. At the national level, we must carefully select our lawmakers and our government as the future of upholding our constitution is in their hands.

Courts are usually considered above legislative bodies in terms of structural authority and the only way to reverse the highest court in a jurisdiction is by executive order, which is rarely exercised. For example, if a death sentence in India were to be reversed, only the president has the executive powers to do so. In different countries the executive order rests with different offices.

096 | News and the media: How to focus in a frenzy?

One important change that has taken place in the last few decades is the rise of the media fraternity which has kept a strong check on all key institutions. From women's empowerment to racism, from corruption to black money, from crime to mis-governance, the media holds all authorities accountable.

There are debates on all global issues – such as climate change, animal conservation, poverty, health, literacy, human rights issues, etc. – that people now think about largely due to media intervention. Fierce debates are held in India on key issues, helping people open their eyes to truths they have often wondered about. Digital media and social media are arenas for heated debates and discussions.

In an era of multiple news sources, the challenge is to filter noise and perceive news from a neutral perspective. Various news houses have a bias against a particular political party or person or have an agenda while speaking to the public. This is wrong, and people must learn to filter such noise. One must see an apple for an apple. I usually read news on Twitter and go through the articles that interest me. I broadly skim the headlines in print newspapers and read articles that are of value to me. Whenever I get time, I choose to scroll through the news websites I have subscribed to. I watch the headlines on TV too – usually over dinner – and find that the usual intake of news in a single day is larger today than it once was.

The one group of people who appear in the news the most are politicians. They often speak with a vote-gaining agenda and people should be aware that this is useless jargon aimed to hit out at political opponents. A lot of what they say can be propaganda that is aimed to aggressively retaliate against claims made by opponents. Citizens should learn to form their own views and not blindly believe any media house. The credibility of media houses is established over a period of neutral reporting and smart consumers are the ones that decide that.

President Donald Trump had waged a literal war on news houses that supposedly reported 'fake news'. This was a bold battle as almost all politicians succumb to the media to try and be in their good books. But should they? There is power in truth. So much so that no one can take away your reputation or your civil liberties in most countries.

Clear, crisp and informative news should be read, and the rest should be discarded as noise. News shouldn't be allowed to become a medium for newsmakers to brainwash people too. It usually isn't, but here is still noise that needs to be kept out. We wouldn't be a hundred per cent safe in our houses without the force of the media and its contribution to causing change, believe me.

097 | Who is driving our system towards perfection on a daily basis?

We often salute our men and women in uniform. But being in politics is just as tough as serving in the army and it's also a service rendered to a nation. That's why we should respect 'idealistic leaders' as well. Politicians are said to be power-hungry people but in reality they too are serving the people of their country and that too usually on a meagre salary. The power they wield comes inadvertently with the position they hold. They are servants of society, there to make things better for you if you let them.

Politicians and civil servants face immense public scrutiny. It's a tough task. To govern well and then fight elections over and over again as well as be liable for mistakes – sometimes made by others – is something I can't imagine doing. I really admire people who take this up as a full-time career.

Civil servants, often known as bureaucrats, work on small salaries too. Their role is powerful and respectable, but as the polity calls the shots in many countries, they are often not the lawmakers. Sometimes, of course, they function independently, but this happens only in an ideal system. We see the judiciary as more powerful than the political class, as they are independent and can supersede the latter. These two bodies control the minds and actions of the government and civil servants. There is immense responsibility on the media and judiciary, as they are the bodies to look up to when there is a crisis in the country and hope ceases to exist

One issue that many countries experience is corruption. The whole system becomes rusty because of this one problem. From the top of the hierarchy to the very bottom, corruption prevails and prohibits development. Countries like this tend to remain the poorest, as everything is affected by the corrupt officials and public money doesn't trickle down to benefit those that it is intended to.

For the system to function ideally, the people must vote smartly to elect the right people. The people must raise their voices, get educated and send their children to schools and universities. That is the way out for countries rife with corruption. Change will take place slowly and steadily, and with that will come prosperity and abundance.

098| Which global forums stand out?

Standards need to be set high so that the world continues to want to achieve them. Since childhood, we have seen competition to get into the best schools, the best colleges and so on. What happens after that? Where does the competitive spirit go? It exists but instead of existing in the microcosmic worlds we used to live in, it expands to fit the real world. A cab driver in Pittsburgh once told me, 'The world is all yours, it depends on what you make of it'. To make an impact on this world, you have to first prove your mettle.

International forums like the World Economic Forum (WEF) challenge us at the national level and set high standards for all nations to achieve. There are many other forums like the WEF, such as the Young Presidents' Organization (YPO), Federation of Indian Chambers of Commerce & Industry (FICCI), Confederation of Indian Industry (CII), etc. in India and all over the world. Key issues relating to the world and the country are discussed in these forums that are typically for businessmen. Ideas and issues affecting us daily are discussed in such forums. It is a get-together of brains, combining and putting forth ideas about a range of issues. People, however, doubt the effectiveness of the World Economic Forum and other such bodies – like the ones I mentioned – and if they can cause change or not. Even if, hypothetically, they can't, they at least provide an environment for people to learn, socialize and exchange viewpoints.

Another esteemed body that is challenging people and organizations to strive higher is the Nobel Foundation– set up by Alfred Nobel in 1895. People or organizations from various fields are awarded medals, cash and certificates every year in the month of October. There is also the Nobel Prize. These prizes are given to high achievers and a lot of academics and intellectuals dream of being given this accolade. You will see that there is a direct correlation between Nobel Laureates and the rankings of the universities they went to, indicating high IQ and impact.

Another esteemed institution is the Giving Pledge started by Bill Gates and Warren Buffet, where billionaires pledge half or more of their wealth to charity. They have no obligation to do so immediately but can do so at a future date or in their will. They can pledge to give to any cause or to multiple causes. Before the pandemic, they had over 180 signatories from 22 countries, with pledges totalling USD 365 billion.

There are many more such bodies and organizations that are setting higher standards of conduct for us. I have only talked about the few among them that stand out as my favourites.

Wikimedia Foundation deserves a special mention for providing a one-stop shop encyclopaedia for free and not for profit. They are truly raising the bar for service to humanity.

099| Why is suffrage important?

Having spent most of my adult life overseas, I voted for the first time in the Maharashtra state elections in 2014. Voting is a powerful tool for people in any democracy and allows them to make a difference. Democracy, I believe, is the best system of governance as we see various forms of 'stifling' or oppression in cases of pure anarchy or communism. I am glad I live in a democratic state where the leaders are answerable to the people and where they have to woo voters to be re-elected. Every grievance of the country is taken seriously. I might sound like a sadistic voter but it's important to make sure our country is well-run. I am glad for the media and the judicial system and their power to bring lawbreakers to justice.

During election time, vote-hunters from all political parties begin their campaigns and here people hold them accountable for their past and extract promises for a brighter future. Today is the age of the wise voter who is privy to information, in almost real time. Elected officials know they cannot sit back and let anything slide during their term in office, as the voter is an aware citizen. If they slip in some way, they or their party will not return to power as people have lots of options to choose from.

During election time, one must vote and get others to vote too. It is this right of suffrage that makes democracies function and determines whether a country is a success or a failure. Do not be lackadaisical about exercising your most fundamental constitutional right.

100 | Do those who are weaker have to try harder to put forth their point?

We often have underlying belief systems and modes of thinking that have developed since our birth and our first interactions with the outside world. These vary and are unique to every individual. Such belief systems often carry prejudices and biases that might be racist, Islamophobic or misogynistic. Women are often subject to such biases and unequal treatment. Fanaticism, colonialism and barbarism of past ages are gradually being replaced by rationalism, democracy and fair legal systems.

A watertight system is compromised through its few weaknesses, such as discrimination, corruption and exploitation. The recent case of George Floyd is devastating, and a much-needed eye-opener to the prejudices and oppressive behaviours that still exist in the world.

Empowerment, awareness, funding, equal opportunities and education – we have to make these accessible for any demographic that has been left behind. This objective should be a part of corporate philosophies, philanthropy, state policies and NGO work. A huge workforce composed of social media activists is working hard to accelerate global action to get rid of pre-existing prejudices and beliefs. One day Islam won't be linked to terror, we will see a prosperous Africa, there will be no corruption and, if we are lucky, there will be more racially diverse billionaires featured on the Forbes list. We live in a capitalistic world, which has salience, but sentiments drive the world.

101 | How has technology interfered with human evolution?

Various kinds of institutions and organizations exist: educational, financial, commercial, political, judicial, governmental, non-governmental and so on. In an age where people crave for identity through affiliations, we forget that there could be life beyond the brands that define us, be it our college or organization, country or state, surname or designation.

Human minds can be conditioned to work under constructs, but these can chain us down or set us free depending on how we choose to live. The choice is ours. Simplification is key. Competition forces us to draw our identity from the entities we are affiliated to, and that is fine for bad times, but to live is to enjoy every second of our life, and only then can we realize our full potential and establish bonds that give life meaning. We have to simplify our mental schemas as much as possible and channel our cognitive abilities to achieve something ahead of time and build a future. A global outlook can be better than belonging to a faction. Our affiliations are our assets, our knowledge and experience our strength, but to put weight on something that isn't your present is living in your comfort zone forever. It could be something one does when they are idle, just for introspection and as a tool to go achieve higher quality quotients, such as happiness and prosperity.

Being patriotic or showing pride in our college degrees or the organizations we are associated with is well and good. However, as necessary as the right alignment is, one can forego opportunities for obtaining new insights through this route. Why be constrained by boundaries and narrowed horizons? The future asks us to get rid of groupthink, build a positive ethos and, with the internet, drive positive change. We are a small world, and can transcend the distance between different geographies through a face-to-face video call. How much quicker is today's world compared to our forefathers', where the people could work much more slowly because of a lack of conveniences? There was discipline, routine and an emphasis on simpler things. Can we have the same mental peace now, with a smartphone and 24x7 internet connectivity? Are we becoming slaves to technology? Are we becoming conformists?

There is no doubt in my mind that technology is a driver of human evolution. Will it affect our progeny's sanity? Height? Weight? Cognitive abilities? Depending on technology has made us more lethargic, and the information we consume has increased multifold. Thus, our mind works overtime and our body less than it should. That sounds like too much to take for our nervous system. To avoid getting overwhelmed with this excess information, we have to set our schemas free, or in simple words, declutter.

Years ago, there was more physical labour to be done as weaker technology meant more physical effort. Those were times with lower mental stress but a life without answers. The internet and so many other means of knowledge didn't exist, after all!

Strike a balance. Reach across boundaries, be positive about competition and attract soft power through actions and words. Fewer complexities are possible through a decent balance between work and life and greater assimilation.

What is life? According to me, it's every moment spent enjoying what you do. And if you find this enjoyment in your work, you have found life in the best possible way! Live, laugh, love and spread joy, for we have reached a point where the average human age is increasing. Things may be headed in the right direction. Obviously, everything isn't hunky dory, but maybe if we bridge the loopholes of all aberrations coming about due to excessive and accelerating changes, we may just reach better and higher milestones in health and shared prosperity. Artificial intelligence (AI), blockchains, the metaverse and the entire Web 3.0 have just made their mark. Let's see how it unfolds.

ACKNOWLEDGEMENTS

This book would not have been possible but for the support of my near-and-dear ones, both family and friends, who encouraged me throughout the process of writing and gave me their feedback. I would like to thank my father for giving me a free hand in business and in my personal life, my mother who supports me in whatever I set out to do and my sister who has so much love to give, along with the love of her life, Sunny, who is like a brother to me. My paternal grandfather deserves a special mention, as he has been a pillar of strength for the entire family and has written five Hindi poetry books, which inspired me tremendously. My maternal grandfather always encouraged me to read as a youngster and would take me to bookshops himself. He still reads daily and it is he who brought me back on track whenever I wandered astray in life. Both Dadi and Nani are special, and I know they will be proud of this book. I have two gems in my life, my maternal and paternal uncles, who have tremendous faith in me, and their presence in my life is enough to achieve things. My friends and cousins are accommodating individuals who listen to me non-stop. Some of them deserve to be mentioned, but I will stay away from that territory, as others will feel left out. But please know that I thought of you while writing this book. Lastly, I would like to thank my professors, educators and teachers in all stages of life to have enabled me to achieve and think as I do. Thank you very much, truly.

ABOUT THE AUTHOR

Vaibhav Maloo has been Managing Director of the Enso Group since 2009. His sharp business vision and strategic bent of mind earned him a crucial and well deserved promotion early in his career. Vaibhav holds a BSc in Business Administration from Carnegie Mellon University and a PgD in Global Business from the University of Oxford. Having worked in multiple cities globally, he also has extensive experience as a traveller. Vaibhav has been a columnist with leading magazines and newspapers in India, and his articles can be found on his website, www.vaibhavmaloo.com.